JAGUAR E-TYPE

JAGUAR E-TYPE

The Complete Story

Jonathan Wood

First published in 1990 by
The Crowood Press Ltd
Ramsbury, Marlborough,
Wiltshire SN8 2HR

Paperback Edition 1998

British Library Cataloguing-in-Publication Data

Wood, Jonathan
 E-type Jaguar.
 1. Jaguar E-type cars, history
 I. Title
 629.2′222

 ISBN 1 86126 1470

The photographs in this book were kindly supplied by The
Motoring Picture Library, Beaulieu.

The line drawings on pages 25, 30, 62, 63, 70, 83, 102, 103, 136,
137, 145, 174, and 175 were drawn by Nino Acanfora; the
photographs on pages 10, 13, 47, 111, 122, 129, 135, 149 and 150
are reproduced courtesy of Jaguar Cars and those on pages 176,
177, 179, 180 and 181 are reproduced courtesy of Paul Skilleter.

Typeset by Footnote Graphics, Warminster, Wiltshire.
Printed and bound by Times Offset, Malaysia.

Contents

Early E-type: a 1961 3.8-litre roadster, fitted with the optional hard-top that subsequently became available, from May 1962, and endured throughout the production life of the Series I and II cars.

Acknowledgements

The majority of the original black and white photographs in this Crowood AutoClassic comes from the National Motor Museum's Beaulieu photographic library and I am also grateful to Jaguar Cars and Paul Skilleter for providing additional pictures.

My thanks are due to Bob Murray, editor of *Autocar & Motor*, for his permission to reproduce E-type road tests from past issues of *Autocar* and *Motor* magazines. I am also grateful for the assistance provided by Arnold Bolton of Jaguar Cars.

Also the clubs, namely Rosemary Hinton (Jaguar Drivers' Club) Gordon Wright (Jaguar Enthusiasts' Club) and John Bridcutt (Jaguar Car Club) kindly provided information about their respective organisations. Thanks are also due to Colin Ford, E-type technical adviser to the Jaguar Enthusiasts' Club, for advice on some of the practical aspects of E-type ownership.

If you're a past, present, prospective E-type owner, or just like classic cars, I trust that you'll be interested in what follows.

Jonathan Wood

THE JAGUAR E-TYPE IN CONTEXT

Prototypes

December 1956	Work underway on '2.4-litre two-seater': what will become the E-type
15 May 1957	Prototype E-type, unofficially designated E1A, tested at the Motor Industry Research Association (MIRA)
July 1958	Second (Pearl Grey) E-type prototype running
July 1959	Three E-type prototypes, E1A, Pearl Grey and Cotswold Blue cars, being evaluated
27 February 1960	E2A sports-racer completed

The E-Type

15 March 1961	E-type launched on Press Day at Geneva Show
October 1964	4.2-litre E-type launched at London Motor Show
March 1966	2 + 2 E-type launched
11 July 1966	Jaguar announces that it will merge with the British Motor Corporation to form British Motor Holdings
14 May 1968	British Motor Holdings merges with Leyland Motor Corporation to form British Leyland Motor Corporation
October 1968	Series II E-type launched at London Motor Show
July 1969	William Heynes retires as Jaguar's chief engineer
July 1970	Malcolm Sayer dies
March 1971	Series III E-type launched
3 March 1972	Sir William Lyons retires as chairman of Jaguar Cars and becomes its president. He is replaced by F R W 'Lofty' England
6 October 1973	Start of 'Yom Kippur' war
16 October 1973	Gulf States announce seventeen per cent rise in oil prices, so triggering a world recession
January 1974	'Lofty' England announces his retirement
9–13 September 1974	The last E-type built during this working week
27 November 1974	British Leyland meets Department of Industry and banks as it is expected to reach the limit of its £152 million overdraft facility in December
18 December 1974	Government commissions Ryder Report
February 1975	Jaguar announces E-type to cease production

1 The Right Company

'There is nothing more typically English than the Jaguar and Sir William Lyons is the typical Englishman.'

The Motor, 15 March 1961

There are few who would argue that the E-type Jaguar is the most significant British sports car of the post-war years. Derived from the Le Mans winning D-type, it was also the fastest road-going Jaguar of its day and the firm's most numerically successful two-seater. Not only was the car competitively priced but, above all, the E-type could only have been a Jaguar, such was the sheer beauty and assurance of its unique lines. The E-type was a head turner when it was new. It still is today.

Yet, ironically, this most memorable car was one of the few Jaguars not to have been styled by the company's shrewd, talented chairman, Sir William Lyons. That accolade must go to the firm's aerodynamicist, Malcolm Sayer – who also has the D's lines to his credit – while chief engineer William Heynes was responsible for its sophisticated and unique mechanical structure. When Jaguar introduced its E-type in 1961, it represented the ultimate expression of a line that had begun, back in 1934, when the newly formed S.S. Cars introduced its first sports car.

THE SWALLOW SIDECAR COMPANY

The S.S. name is rooted in the Swallow Sidecar Company established in 1922 Black-pool, where William Lyons' father ran a piano sales business. William Lyons teamed up with William Walmsley, who had designed a stylish Zeppelin-shaped motor cycle side-car under the Swallow name. It was decided to expand Walmsley's business, which had hitherto been confined to his garden shed, and the firm prospered. In 1927, the Swallow Sidecar *and Coachbuilding* Company diversified by taking an existing car and bodying it with more fashionable coachwork. The first model to benefit from this approach was the popular but utilitarian Austin Seven because, Lyons believed '. . . that it would also appeal to a lot of people if it had a more luxurious and attractive body'. This was a distinctive open tourer, with its own cowled radiator, and was followed in 1928 by a stylish saloon.

The young company had a number of locations during its formative years and Lyons, who had emerged as the dominating personality within the partnership, decided that the business should leave Blackpool and move to the very heart of the motor industry in the city of Coventry. This had been forced on the firm after Lyons had obtained an order from Henlys for 500 Austin Swallows when the factory was only capable of producing two cars a day! He discovered a former Shell filling plant in the Foleshill district of Coventry, at Whitmore

Sir William Lyons, creator of the SS and Jaguar marques, poses at Wappenbury Hall with a 'Series I½' left-hand drive E-type coupe of the 1967–1968 era. He much preferred the closed version to that of the roadster.

Park – later named Swallow Road – and the move was effected between October and November 1928. The firm's floor space having grown fivefold, Swallow production could be upped from twelve to fifty cars per week. Also, other makes were offered with special coachwork, namely Standard, Swift, Wolseley and Fiat chassis.

But Lyons was not content with pursuing a secondary, coachbuilding role. He wanted to become a car manufacturer in his own right and the outcome was the S.S.1 coupe, which appeared at the very depths of the depression at the 1931 London Motor Show. Its low, very French lines and long bonnet were impressive enough but so was its £310

Sir William Lyons (1901–1985)

Immaculate in a dark suit, Lyons was, by the E-type years, the highest paid executive in British industry, with a salary of £100,000 a year. He also possessed a flair for appointing talented subordinates, whom he persisted in addressing by their surnames. Sir William was enigmatic, cautious, financially canny, and above all, a supreme stylist. Although he drew on continental and American design influences for his cars, he always managed to create the distinctive and stylish 'Jaguar look' and this usually ensured a long production run, which kept costs down. When it came to styling exercises, Lyons rarely relied on scale models but opted instead for full size mock-ups. These were often photographed against the background of Wappenbury Hall, near Leamington Spa, where he lived the life of the country gentleman and was proud of his prize-winning herd of Suffolk sheep.

Ironically, Sir William was not responsible for the lines of his most memorable sports car, the E-type. These were the work of aerodynamicist Malcolm Sayer. In fact, Lyons was always a little lukewarm about the model. Although it has been suggested that this was because he had not created its memorable lines, the real reason must surely be that SS, and later Jaguar, was essentially a manufacturer of saloon cars, with the low production sports models playing second fiddle to them in terms of volume, and thus profitability. Significantly, the XJ6, a saloon, was his all-time favourite Jaguar.

Lyons always ran a 'tight ship', It was an approach perhaps best recalled by an incident that occurred at Browns Lane during a winter when the factory, and its grounds, were covered with a deep fall of snow. 'Lofty' England took the opportunity of getting some of Jaguar's employees to clear snow away from the office block in anticipation of Sir William's arrival. When Lyons did appear, he told England: 'That's very kind of you – well done. But what do the men do normally – how is it that we can spare them?'

selling price. The multi-faceted Lyons was a proprietor who individually styled his own products. These usually enjoyed long production runs, so helping to keep the selling price down.

In the first instance however, the S.S.1's mechanicals did not complement its striking bodywork. The low coupe concealed a special Standard Ensign-derived chassis and was available with 2- or 2.5-litre six-cylinder Standard side-valve engines. In its larger capacity form, the S.S.1 could manage 75mph (120kph) on a good day. As for the S.S. name, Lyons was involved in lengthy discussions with Standard, from whom he bought his engines, and later recounted: 'There was much speculation whether S.S. stood for Standard Swallow or Swallow Special – it was never resolved.'

A much improved S.S.1, with new underslung chassis, followed for 1933 and, in 1935, came the S.S.90, which was Lyons' first true sports car. This was an open two-seater with the long stylish wings for which S.S. was soon to be so famous. The S.S.90 was based on a shortened S.S.1 chassis, though under the heavily louvred bonnet there was still a Standard side-valve of 2,663cc, but with a high lift camshaft and a 7:1 compression ratio. It was reckoned that the car was capable of speeds approaching 90mph (144kph) which gave the model its name. And like its XK and E-type descendants, it was competitively priced: the S.S.90 sold for £395. In other words you could have bought two S.S.90s for about the price of a top-line 1½-litre Aston Martin. Despite this, only twenty-three examples were sold – discriminating buyers no doubt recognising the limitations of its side-valve power.

No one was more aware of this shortcoming than Lyons himself and he had various thoughts about improving the performance of his cars. The fitment of a Studebaker engine had been contemplated (Henlys had an agency for the make), and a Zoller supercharger was considered. Then Lyons

The pointers to the E-type's lines can be seen in the Malcolm Sayer-styled C-type, built to win Le Mans, which it did first time out, in 1951. Here Stirling Moss, in XKC053, is pictured at Le Mans in 1953.

had the good fortune to discover tuning specialist Harry Weslake, who greeted him with the words: 'Your car reminds me of an overdressed lady with no brains – there's nothing under the bonnet.' Weslake began work on an overhead valve conversion for the long suffering 2.6-litre Standard unit. This culminated in an impressive rise from about 75 to 105bhp. But what S.S. required was a proper engineering section and, in April 1935, Lyons appointed thirty-one year old William Heynes from Humber as chief engineer and one man development department!

Heynes was given the formidable task of getting a new saloon car range ready for the Motor Show six months later. The point must be made at this stage that S.S., and its Jaguar successor, has primarily been a manufacturer of saloon cars, with the more dramatic and memorable sports cars always

playing second fiddle to them in numerical, and thus profitable, terms. The new SS Jaguar range duly appeared at the 1935 Show and was also significant for the downgrading of the SS name, which lost its full stops, and the arrival of the Jaguar one. Lyons had asked, what he later described as his 'publicity department', in other words his hard-working publicity manager, Bill Rankin, to come up with a list of bird, animal and fish names and Lyons '... immediately pounced on Jaguar because it had an exciting sound to me'. He also remembered a friend working on a Siddeley Jaguar aero engine during World War I.

This pivotal year of 1935 also saw the new Weslake converted engine fitted under the bonnet of the SS90 sports car, which gloried in the memorable SS100 name – a reflection of its brake horsepower rather than top speed. Acceleration was a notable improvement on that of the 90 and the car was capable of 90mph (144kph) plus. From 1938 the SS Jaguar saloons were fitted with an enlarged 3.5-litre engine, which was also made available to the SS100, making it a true 100mph (160kph) car. The model was soon making its mark in competition and, in 1937, won the team prize in that year's RAC Rally. The SS100 remained in production until 1941, by which time 308 examples had been completed.

With the outbreak of war in 1939, Lyons, still only thirty-eight, could look back on a decade of unparalleled growth: SS had just built a record 5,378 cars and, following the 1933 creation of S.S. Cars Ltd, two years later the firm had become a public company. However, William Walmsley had retired in 1934, which left Lyons as undisputed head of the firm. In addition to his outstanding stylistic abilities, Lyons had shown himself to be a shrewd judge of men. Key appointments had included Heynes as chief engineer; Arthur Whittaker, whose association with the firm reached back to its Blackpool roots, as purchasing manager; and in 1938, the engineering team was strengthened by the arrival of the talented Walter Hassan, who had worked for Bentley, ERA and Thomson and Taylor at Brooklands, prior to joining SS as chief experimental engineer.

THE RIGHT NAME – THE RIGHT MOVES

During hostilities, SS Cars repaired Whitley aircraft fuselages and manufactured them

William Heynes, Jaguar's outstanding chief engineer, who was responsible for the overall conception of the E-type, pictured on the production line with a left-hand drive roadster.

William Munger Heynes, (1903–1989)

Unquestionably the most influential man in the Jaguar company after Sir William himself, Heynes joined SS as chief engineer in 1935 and became engineering director and vice-chairman in 1961. Initially only assisted by a single draughtsman, Heynes later built up the Jaguar engineering department to be one of the most respected in the industry. In addition, he played a significant role in the creation of the XK engine and his C-type won Le Mans first time out in 1951, laying the foundations for Jaguar's racing reputation that endures to this day. It was followed by the sports-racing D and, finally, the most memorable of all Jaguar's sports cars, the E-type.

One of a family of six boys, Leamington Spa-born Heynes attended nearby Warwick Public School and there his science master tried to encourage him to become a surgeon, though the lengthy and necessary training was beyond his family's resources.

But the medical profession's loss was the motor industry's gain. In 1923 he joined Humber as an apprentice, moved to the design office in 1925 and remained with the Coventry company for a further ten years. It says much for Heynes' abilities that, from 1930 onwards, he was put in charge of the firm's technical department.

Heynes joined SS Cars in April 1935, and remained with the firm until his retirement in 1969, and while he respected Lyons for his undoubted achievements, he probably knew him better than most, and has left us his observations of the Jaguar chairman, which are both perceptive and candid. On joining SS, he found his young boss, who was only two years his senior, straight talking, lacking a 'light touch' and a sense of humour. Lyons also expected those around him to work the same long hours as he did. Some time after Heynes joined SS, he asked Lyons whether he might take a holiday. Lyons responded sharply, 'Why, are you ill?' Heynes replied, 'No but I haven't had a holiday for two years!' Heynes became a director in 1946 but thought that the Jaguar board meetings were '... a real joke. He [Lyons] just said what he wanted to do and everyone agreed with him – except,' says Heynes, 'me'.

for another bomber, the Stirling, as well as for the Meteor – Britain's first operational jet. But these years were not solely concerned with such work, as Lyons and his team were planning a new 100mph (160kph) saloon for what they saw as the challenge of the post-war era.

In these all-important discussions – which took place in the small development department – Lyons, Heynes and Hassan were joined by Claude Baily, former assistant chief designer of Morris Motors, who had arrived in 1940 to take charge of engine design development. As the Standard-based engines were clearly reaching the end of their production life, the team's aim was to produce a power unit which, in Heynes' words, would '... need to be capable of propelling a full size saloon at a genuine 100mph in standard form and without special tuning'. Although a four-cylinder, V8, six and even a V12 were considered, the team eventually decided that to produce the necessary 160bhp, an engine with a high-efficiency hemispherical cylinder head, with inclined overhead valves, would have to be employed. From 1943 experimental units were built, all prefixed X for Experimental.

The XF was a 1,360cc four to prove the viability of the concept. The XG was, in effect, a 1,996cc Standard four fitted with a cross pushrod head of the type used so successfully on the pre-war BMW 328 sports car – though this proved to be excessively noisy when tested in a saloon. The XJ was an 80×98mm 1,996cc four and many of the experiments with port and head design were undertaken on this unit. The XJ prefix was also used on the first six-cylinder and was intended to replace the existing 2.5- and 3.5-litre engines with a single unit. However, it was found that it suffered from poor low speed torque and, at Harry Weslake's suggestion, the stroke was increased from 98 to 106mm while the bore remained at 83mm, giving a capacity of 3,448cc. An aluminium cylinder head was standardised while at the other end of the unit, the substantial crankshaft ran in seven main bearings. This became the definitive XK engine while the 1,996cc four-cylinder version was also readied for production.

But the still small SS company was sailing in uncharted waters because the twin overhead camshaft engine had previously been confined to high performance sports and touring cars in the manner of the Italian Alfa Romeo or Bugatti from France. The only British twin-cam to have been built in any numbers had been the 1,098cc Lagonda Rapier sports car of the 1934–1939 vintage (about 250 examples had been made). And from Lyons' standpoint, the twin overhead XK engine had an added bonus in that it also *looked* good. Like Ettore Bugatti, he was a great believer in the merits of underbonnet artistry. This, then, was the engine on which the firm's post-war fortunes were to be built and it not only powered the projected big saloon but also the sports car line which culminated in the E-type.

With the coming of peace in 1945, Lyons was the first to recognise that the SS initials had become tarnished by their identification with the fanatical Nazi élite: 'A sector of the community which was not highly regarded' was how he later put it. So in April 1945, the month before the war in Europe ended, SS Cars became Jaguar Cars, a name which Lyons had prudently registered back in November 1937.

Jaguar had not restarted sports car production after the war but instead concentrated, from August 1945, on a mildly updated version of its 1938 saloon range of Standard-engined 1.5-, 2.5- and 3.5-litre cars. But post-war Britain was urgently in need of foreign currency and steel allocation was geared to export performance. Like the rest of the British motor industry, Jaguar had exported few cars pre-war, and the 1939 record figures only amounted to a mere 252 examples. Yet in the economically chilly post-war world, along with the rest of the

British motor industry, Jaguar looked for the first time to a world market. As Lyons later remembered: 'We set out to convince the Government that the models we had coming along would command a substantial export market.' The firm's export programme was carefully itemised and Lyons personally delivered this '... very elaborate brochure ... to Sir George Turner, who was then Permanent Secretary to the Ministry of Supply, and I elaborated verbally on our plans and obtained his promise of support. Within two weeks we received a permit for the full quota of steel for which we had asked.'

This commitment paved the way for an aggressive export programme. Jaguar cars were offered with left-hand steering for the first time in 1947 when about a quarter of output was sent overseas. Initially, cars went to such established empire markets as Australia, New Zealand and South Africa, but it was America which responded most positively to the Jaguar. However, the opening-up of this new transatlantic market eliminated the need for the smaller four-cylinder XK engine which was accordingly sidelined.

Although Jaguar's first objective had been to develop a new 100mph (160kph) saloon (it finally appeared as the Mark VII in 1950), there was clearly a need for a stop-gap model. This appeared at the 1948 London Motor Show in the shape of the Mark V saloon range.

The Mark V, outwardly similar to its predecessor, had a new box section chassis which featured a Citroen-inspired torsion bar independent front-suspension system, designed pre-war by William Heynes, to replace the half elliptics used hitherto. But sharing Jaguar's stand at the 1948 Motor Show was Jaguar's new sports car, a magnificent bronze-coloured XK120, powered by the 3.4-litre twin overhead camshaft engine that had been developed for the big Mark VII saloon, which was still two years away.

Sir William Lyons (centre) inspects the cockpit of the D-type (XKC402) prior to the 1954 Le Mans race. Note the forward-opening bonnet and triangulated front framework, both features which were perpetuated on the E-type. The oil tank for the dry-sump oil system is in the foreground.

The XK120

The XK120 was based on a shortened version of the Mark V's chassis and its lovely lines were inspired by a special open BMW 328 sports car, run by the German company in the 1940 Mille Miglia race. That particular BMW was brought to Britain after hostilities by H J Aldington, the pre-war importer of BMW cars, and loaned to the industry for evaluation. One of the firms to examine the 328 was Jaguar, as it was a model which Lyons held in high regard, and he was able to use its lines as the basis for his new sports car. But the XK120, so named to respectively reflect its engine and top speed, was also significant in another dimension. It represented a milestone in British sports car design as a comfortable, well-equipped car which flew in the face of its stark, back-jarring predecessors. The model was in instant demand, particularly in America, and the car's success took Jaguar by surprise. The first 240 examples were aluminium-bodied and hand-built in the customary pre-war coachbuilding traditions. Consequently, Pressed Steel took over responsibility for the XK120's body which became an all-steel structure.

This model, in turn, led Jaguar to the famous and demanding Le Mans 24-hour race, which had restarted after the war in

Chief engineer William Heynes at the wheel of the unpainted prototype D-type (XKC401), at Browns Lane in April 1954. Later registered OVC 501, the car was used for testing and evaluating a De Dion rear axle.

1949. For the 1950 event, three basically standard XK120s, unofficially sponsored by the factory, were entered. Two of them finished 12th and 15th, but although the third dropped out with clutch trouble in the 21st hour, it was in third place at the time, which convinced Lyons that: 'In a car more suitable for the race, the XK engine could win this greatest of all events.'

The decision to enter an official Jaguar works team at Le Mans was not taken until October 1950 – the publicity benefits of a win there being enormous. But there were other reasons for entering a team of cars for the event and I can do no better than to quote Robert (Bob) Berry, a Jaguar employee of the day, who raced a lightweight XK120 himself and advised others who wanted to do the same. In 1976, Berry reflected that:

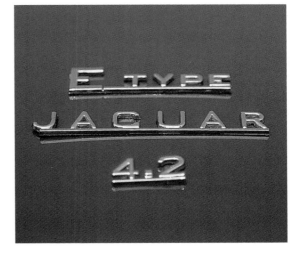

The 3.8-litre E-type just had the word 'Jaguar' on its rear but, by the time the 4.2 had arrived in 1964, it was so identified and 'E-type' was later added.

'In retrospect three factors made the decision to continue inevitable. The first, and most obvious, was the degree of success achieved to date with relatively little in technical and financial resources. Secondly the [1950] Le Mans foray had shown that even the most respected names were far from invincible but thirdly, and overridingly, was the conclusion that the ever increasing level of opposition from full factory teams participating in relatively small events, was at last sounding the death knell in the era of the private owner.'

ON THE WAY TO THE E: JAGUAR'S SPORTS RACING LINE

The C-Type

The 'more suitable' car of which Lyons had spoken was William Heynes' C-type. Its creation marks the starting point of a commission which evolved into the D-type and, ultimately, the E-type. A team of three Cs were rapidly prepared for the 1951 race. The intention was to produce a faster, lighter, more powerful version of the XK120 with a new, aerodynamically-improved body. All these objectives were met. In its roadster form, the XK120 was a 124mph (199kph) car, while the C-type could achieve 143mph (230kph). The XK120 turned the scales at 27cwt (1,371kg) while the C-type weighed considerably less at 20cwt (1,016kg). The XK engine developed 160bhp in the road car and developed 44 more at 204bhp in the sports-racer, while the sleek body lines were a considerable improvement on those of the production model.

Precious pounds were saved by Heynes adopting a multi-tubular space frame chassis. Front-suspension was essentially the XK120's independent torsion bar system though, at the rear, there was a considerable departure from standard: the half elliptic springs were replaced by a single transversely-mounted torsion bar, connected to the live rear axle by trailing arms, while torque reaction members prevented lateral movement. Rack and pinion steering gear was a first for any Jaguar car. The C-type's wheelbase was shorter than the XK120's, being 8ft (2.44m) rather than the 8ft 6in (2.85m) of the road car.

The engines used in the XK120s entered for the 1950 Le Mans race were carefully prepared for the event but were basically standard units. In the C, high lift camshafts were introduced, along with enlarged inlet valves. The inlet manifold was larger and 2in (50mm) SU carburetters replaced 1.75in (44mm) units. The compression ratio was upped from 8 to 9:1.

The creation of the C-type's bodywork was the first assignment tackled by thirty-four year old Malcolm Sayer, an aerodynamicist from the Bristol Aeroplane Company who had joined Jaguar in 1950. Sayer's brief was to design an aerodynamically more efficient body while still being identifiably related to the XK120. The aluminium body which resulted was produced in three sections, with the bonnet hinging at its forward end while the rear could be easily detached to reveal the rear-suspension.

Although two of the three C-types dropped out of the 1951 Le Mans race, a third, driven by Peters Walker and Whitehead, won the event at a record speed of 93.49mph (150.45kph). It was the first British win at the Sarthe circuit since a Lagonda victory in 1935. The C-type was less lucky in 1952 when last minute alterations to the front of the bodywork resulted in severe overheating and none of the cars finished. The 1953 cars were essentially restatements of the 1951 theme, though they were lighter with 18 rather than 16 gauge tubing. The 220bhp engines sported triple twin choke Weber carburetters, while all-round Dunlop disc brakes, pioneered in competition in the previous year, were employed – as were rubber weight-saving aircraft-type fuel tanks, made by ICI. The 1953 Le Mans race proved to be a copybook event for Jaguar and the C-types came in first, second and fourth.

The 'C/D'

The C-type model was beginning to show its years and in 1953 Heynes and his team produced one example of a new car that can retrospectively be seen as a stepping stone between the C-type and its D-type successor and which also contains the first flickerings of the E-type's sensational body lines. This was chassis XKC 054, which was known as: 'The light alloy chassis XP11.' For many years this car was thought to have a C-type chassis but, according to Bob Berry, Heynes, in his search for reduced weight, was led '... to investigate the advantages of monocoque construction using magnesium alloys

A D-type in action. Duncan Hamilton at the wheel of his car (XKD601) pictured in the 1958 Tourist Trophy race at Goodwood, which marked his retirement from competitive sport. Hamilton shared the driving with Peter Blond and was placed sixth.

Almost certainly the 'Pop-Rivet Special', photographed in 1959.
While the overall E-type shape appears to have been finalised,
much of the body trim has yet to be decided: the air-intake
lacks its decorative bar, there is no chrome trim around the
headlamp covers and no door handles nor permanent
sidelights. The bonnet was secured by an exterior handle in the
manner of the D-type.

for such frame components as there were and, of course, for the body. The techniques of welding structures of this type were in their infancy and to prove both the theory and the practice, a guinea pig was built.'

It was fitted with the engine from the C-type used by Stirling Moss, which was placed fourth in the TT race of the previous month. Malcolm Sayer came up with a new lightweight body, looking lower and smoother than that of the C-type and, in retrospect, very 'D'; particularly around the front end. On 20 October 1953, as a Motor Show pub-

licity exercise, this car was taken to the Jabbeke motorway in Belgium, where it was fitted with a transparent wind-cheating cockpit bubble and, with Jaguar's test driver Norman Dewis at the wheel, clocked 178.3mph (286kph), over the measured mile. In a final run over the flying kilometre, Dewis averaged 179.81mph (289kph); so the XP11 was the first Jaguar ever to exceed 180mph (289kph). However, this achievement was overshadowed by Dewis attaining 172.4mph (277kph) in a specially prepared XK120, also complete with bubble, which

The XK120C 11, retrospectively referred to as the 'C/D-type' at Jabbeke, Belgium, on 20 October 1953. From left to right: Jaguar's aerodynamicist Malcolm Sayer, Jaguar mechanic Len Hayden, driver Norman Dewis, and, checking the front tyre, David 'Dunlop Mac' McDonald.

was the highest speed ever recorded by an XK120.

But impressive as the 'C/D' had been, Heynes and his team were convinced that a completely new sports-racer would be needed if Jaguar was to maintain its Le Mans successes and it was this decision which led to the creation of one of the most legendary sports racing cars of all time: the Jaguar D-type.

The D-Type

If the C-type represented a demonstrable starting point for the E-type project, then the D can be considered to be the source of its structural origins, so its construction is of considerable relevance to our story. Once again the Jaguar design team strove to reduce weight, increase engine power and improve aerodynamics.

The tubular frame of the C-type was dispensed with. Instead Heynes created a monocoque tub of rivetted aluminium panelling – with appropriately-shaped openings for the driver and passenger – which was built-up around two hollow sills with substantial bulkheads front and rear. At the front, the engine/gearbox unit, suspension and steering were carried on what was, in effect, the framework of an oblong box with its four principal members of square section

Malcolm Sayer (1916–1970)

Jaguar's aerodynamicist joined the company in 1950 via that great repository of engineering talent, the Bristol Aeroplane Company. Sayer was responsible for the lines of some of the most famed Jaguar cars of the post-war years, the C- and D-type sports-racers, and the E-type. He also styled (though he never used the word) the still born XJ13 Le Mans car and the current XJ-S.

Born in Cromer, Norfolk, Sayer won a scholarship to Great Yarmouth Grammar School. He received his technical education at Loughborough College and, in 1938, although he had studied automobile engineering, joined the aero engine division of the Bristol Aeroplane Company because it offered better pay and opportunities than the motor industry. Sayer spent the next ten years at Bristol where he became steeped in the world of aerodynamics though cars briefly intruded when he designed the bodywork for the short-lived, locally-built Gordano sports car of 1947. In the following year, he took a job at Baghdad University to establish a chair in engineering, familiarising himself with Arabic on the boat to Iraq. Lack of facilities and political uncertainties resulted in his return to Britain in 1950, and for a job with Jaguar.

Drawing on his experience with Bristol, Sayer was responsible for introducing Jaguar to the world of aerodynamics with its use of wind tunnel facilities and smoke testing. Chief Engineer Heynes considered him: 'A strong and generous character [who] was, nevertheless, quietly spoken and almost unruffled by the turbulence that is characteristic of the car industry.' One of Sayer's favourite stories was when he was flying back from Le Mans with Lyons in a Bristol Freighter, which he knew intimately. Sayer carefully explained to him that the engines were only secured by four 5/16 in (12.7/38.6 cm) bolts. This knowledge rattled the usually imperturbable Lyons, who thoroughly disliked air travel!

Over six feet tall, this charming, talented engineer succumbed to heart disease in 1970 and died at the early age of fifty-four.

magnesium tubing passing through the top front bulkhead and argon arc welded to the rear bulkhead. Additional reinforcement came from a secondary A-shaped frame, mounted on top of it, but anchored to the front rather than to the rear bulkhead. The wishbones and longitudinal torsion bars were essentially carried over from the C at the front while the rear-suspension, though different, was also clearly related to its sports-racer predecessor. The suspension medium was once again a single transversely-located torsion bar and there were four trailing arms forming, in side view, a true parallelogram. Transverse location of the live axle came from an A bracket. As on the C-type, Dunlop disc brakes were fitted front and rear, though the C's wire wheels were not perpetuated but replaced by alloy discs from the same manufacturer. Rack and pinion steering was also retained. With a wheelbase of 7ft 6in (2.29m), the D was 4in (101mm) shorter than the C.

The engine was essentially that of the C-type, though the valves' sizes were increased. The triple Weber carburetters were retained though they were 1.77in (45mm) units rather than the previous year's 1.57in (40mm) ones. With the intention of increasing both engine speeds and bearing loads, a dry-sump lubrication system was employed and, in Heynes' words, '... overcame the disadvantage of having a lot of loose oil floating about inside the engine'. As a result of these ministrations, the D-type's engine developed 240bhp. In the interests of weight saving, there was no flywheel: mass came from a vibration damper mounted on the front of the engine, the clutch, and the flywheel. An aluminium radiator was fitted for the same reason. The engine was mated with a new all-synchromesh gearbox and it is interesting to record that bottom gear synchro did not reach a Jaguar road car until 1965: eleven years later!

When it came to the bodywork, Sayer once again displayed his mastery although, as

One of Malcolm Sayer's visual influences of 1952 was Alfa Romeo's Colombo-designed experimental Disco Volante (Flying Saucer) sports-racer. The wind tunnel-tested body lines were executed for the Milan company by Carrozzeria Touring.

will emerge, the D-type was not quite the aerodynamic *tour de force* that it was considered to be at the time. The D's bodywork was a perpetuation of the lines that Sayer had begun with the so-called 'C/D' of 1953 and it should be recorded that its shape was influenced by the experimental 1952 Alfa Romeo Touring-bodied Disco Volante.

Sayer never considered himself to be a stylist, always an aerodynamicist, and he developed his own unique method of producing a body shape. Stylists usually start with a series of sketches but Sayer's approach was essentially a mathematical one. His starting point was the four parameters of length, width, height and ground clearance. Having fixed these, he would create the car's basic outline, using an elementary formula for an ellipse, and would then produce his lines on a drawing board. Then, once the car's side, plan and head-on views had been created, he would continue to employ the same formula to build up the entire surface of the car. These calculations would then be confirmed by 1:10 scale wind tunnel models.

In applying these methods to create the D-type's lines, he produced one of the most visually impressive cars ever built though, surprisingly, when an early full-sized example was tested in the Royal Aircraft Establishment's Farnborough wind tunnel, it was found to have the not particularly impressive drag coefficient of 0.50, or about the same as the original Volkswagen Beetles! This figure was essentially confirmed in 1982 when *Autocar* magazine submitted the original design's long-nosed successor to testing at the Motor Industry Research Association's (MIRA) wind tunnel where it recorded a figure of 0.489.

Like the C-type's, the D's body was made in three sections: a forward opening bonnet, a centre section and a detachable tail. There was a stabilising rear fin which also concealed the petrol filler cap. The latter fed the twin flexible petrol tanks, containing 37 gallons (168 litres) of fuel, of the type pioneered on the C-type. This helped to contribute to the D's impressive 17cwt (863kg) kerb weight, 3cwt (152kg) less than the C's. Top speed was in excess of 170mph (273kph).

Bob Berry, who raced a privately-entered D, has recorded his impressions of driving this incredible car: 'From my own experience, I can vouch for the fact that, at speeds of over 170mph (273kph), it was possible to sit in the cockpit, relaxed and in relative silence in an envelope of near still air, steering the car with no more pressure than finger and thumb. Especially in the dark the effect was both uncanny and deceptive, the real speed effect coming as a real shock as, on the straight, one rushed past other cars of nominally similar performance.'

A team of three D-types was entered for the 1954 Le Mans race, which developed into a memorable battle between the 4.9-litre Ferrari – driven by Gonzales and Trintignant – and the Jaguar D-type – driven by Duncan Hamilton and Tony Rolt. While the Italian car was able to out-accelerate the 3.4-litre D-type up to 100mph (160kph), the Jaguar was able to steadily draw ahead above that figure. As it happened, the Ferrari won at 105.09mph (169kph) with the Jaguar less than two minutes behind. The other two D-types had dropped out, though a Belgian-entered C was placed fourth.

The 1954 Le Mans race told Jaguar that more power would be needed for 1955. Valves were once again enlarged, though this necessitated redesigning the entire cylinder head, as the exhaust valves – their inclination changed from 35 to 40 degrees – would otherwise have touched the inlets opposite. Higher lift camshafts were also fitted, all of which combined to increase bhp once again: this time to 270.

In addition to these modifications, minor changes were made to the D's structure. The front framework was altered so that its principal members were bolted, rather than welded to the bulkhead. Now only two tubes passed through the monocoque which was similarly bolted in place. This made repairs a far more practical proposition, as it was now possible to detach the power train from the central monocoque with a set of span-

ners. The square section tubes were also changed from magnesium alloy to nickel steel at the same time. Externally, the front of the car was also modified and extended by 7.5in (190mm) to improve airflow. The so-called 'long nose' also incorporated twin air-ducting to the front brakes.

Once the 1955 Le Mans event had begun, it had all the makings of a tremendous tussle between Mike Hawthorn in a D, and Juan Fangio at the wheel of a 300SL Mercedes-Benz, which led for the first nine hours. It quickly became obvious that, while the Jaguar was faster on the straight parts of the course, the Mercedes-Benz's independent rear-suspension gave it the decisive advantage coming out of the corners. However, the event was clouded by the tragic accident which killed eighty-one people and led to the withdrawal of the Mercedes-Benz team soon after 2am on the Sunday morning. This left the Hawthorn/Bueb's D-type to take the lead and it went on to win, with a Belgian-entered D taking third place.

The same year, the factory decided to offer the D for public sale in the manner of its C-type predecessor – a total of forty-three examples having been built for sale in 1952 and 1953. The D was offered at £2,585 in basic form, while British buyers would have to pay £3,663 when purchase tax was added. This put the price of a D on a par with the contemporary sports racing Aston Martin DB3S, which sold for £3,684. By contrast, Jaguar's own XK140 open two-seater cost £1,598 at this time. The D-type continued to be in production until 1957, by which time forty-two had been sold, America being the largest customer.

The 1956 Le Mans cars were much the same as the previous years' though one of them was fitted with a Lucas petrol injection system. The official Jaguar team was dogged by ill fortune however: two of the three cars were eliminated by a crash at the Esses on the third lap, while the fuel-injected Hawthorn/Bueb entry suffered from per-

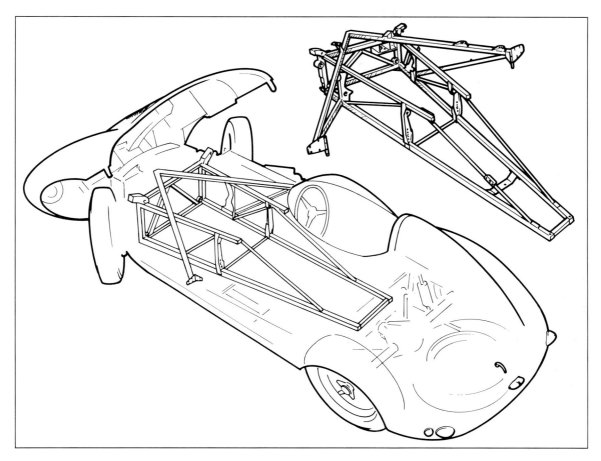

The D-type's front framework of 1955 with the upper members cut short and replaced by angled reinforcement.

sistent misfiring throughout much of the event. This was subsequently traced to a hairline crack in one of the fuel pipes, and eventually the car came in sixth position. But a D-type did take the chequered flag, entered by the Scotland-domiciled Ecurie Ecosse racing stable, with a Belgian-entered D taking fourth place.

On this relatively high note, Jaguar bowed out of competition which, it should be noted, also embraced important British and continental events, in addition to Le Mans. Bob Berry recalls that: 'For all of us closely involved in the programme for over six years, it was indeed a sad day. Interest in

racing by the major manufacturers was in decline and there seemed little enough point in trying to repeat the successes of previous years which, in themselves, created records. The decision was undoubtedly correct and the mantle was passed back to the private teams.'

One such was the famous Edinburgh-based Ecurie Ecosse stable, which continued to campaign the cars; two of which – with enlarged 3.8-litre engines – finished first and second at Le Mans in 1957, with a French-entered D coming third, whilst Belgium once again showed consistency with one of its Ds coming fourth. A British D

This photograph, taken early in 1975, marks the end of the E-type production. The last of the fifty black Series III V12 roadsters (chassis number IS 2872), soon to be registered HDU 555N, is seen on the right with the company's 1953 XK120. Standing from left to right are Jaguar executives Peter Craig, Jack Randle, Alan Currie, and Geoffrey Robinson.

came in sixth. Although Ecurie Ecosse entered Ds again in 1958, 1959 and 1960 it was the end of the road for the model. Since 1951 a Jaguar had won Le Mans on no less than five occasions: a British record only rivalled by Bentley in the 1920s. It made Jaguar a world famous name, particularly in America where the firm sold so many of its cars.

Despite the model's triumphs on the Sarthe circuit, the D was a slow seller. Only thirteen examples had found buyers in 1956 and, in November of that year, the firm still had twenty-nine of them in stock. This prompted the appearance of the road-going D-type, nostalgically titled XKSS, though the familiar initials probably stood for 'Super Sports'. This model went on sale in January 1957 though only one car had been sold by 12 February 1957, when a fire swept through the Jaguar factory and destroyed about half the plant. The XKSS ceased pro-

duction in November, by which time only sixteen cars had been sold, but, more significantly, 1957 was the year in which the first E-type prototype was being evaluated.

ON THE WAY TO THE E: JAGUAR'S SPORTS CAR LINE

Before looking at the E-type's formative evolution, it is first necessary to chart the development of the company's *sports car*, as opposed to *sports racing*, line. It will be recalled that the XK120 had proved its worth in the 1950 Le Mans race though it continued to evolve as a road-going car. A fixed-head version appeared in 1951. The XK120 remained in production until late 1954 when it was replaced by its XK140 derivative after 12,078 XK120s had been built.

The XK140

The XK140 was mechanically similar to the XK120, apart from the fitment of rack and pinion steering. It was available in open, fixed and drop-head coupe forms and is easily identifiable by its wider radiator grille and Mark VII bumpers. In all but the open version, additional rear seats for children were provided.

The heavier XK140 sold somewhat less well than its predecessors and unlike the XK120 – the name of which echoed its top speed – the XK140 did not follow suit: it was capable of 129mph (207kph) in fixed-head form and 8,884 found buyers. Its 135mph (217kph) disc-braked XK150 replacement arrived in 1957 and was available with a similar body range. Up until 1959, all XKs were powered by the 3.4-litre engine which had first appeared in 1948. But in that year came a race-proven 3.8-litre derivative, which was available with a choice of heads: the twin carburettered 220bhp B-type and the S-type, with triple SUs and 265bhp. These options remained available until 1961 when, after thirteen years, the XK line made way for the E-type.

By this time Jaguar was well established in a new home. From the early 1950s, the original factory at Swallow Road, Foleshill, had been proving inadequate for Jaguar's burgeoning growth. As Lyons remembered: 'Although I went to the highest level, we were unable to obtain permission to extend our factory; there was a complete embargo on building in Coventry.' Fortunately for Jaguar, an empty Shadow Factory at Browns Lane, Allesley, on the outskirts of the city – and which had been operated by Daimler during the war – became available. Jaguar was able to buy it and the move was effected between the autumn of 1951 and November 1952. It has been Jaguar's home ever since.

Browns Lane, Allesley, Coventry

Jaguar's home from 1952 to the present day, Browns Lane was one of the original war time shadow factories which peppered the industrial Midlands immediately prior to and during World War II.

The scheme, initiated by the government in 1936, recognised that war with Germany was inevitable and it was decided to dramatically increase the production of Bristol aero engines, which were already in production under licence the world over. The factories would be built at government expense but managed by the Austin, Daimler, Rootes, Rover and Standard car companies. All these firms, with the exception of Austin, were Coventry based and all, apart from Rover's shadow, were located in and around the city. Daimler's factory was built in the grounds of its Radford plant. It was operating from early 1937 but it soon became insufficient for the needs of impending war. So, in the spring of 1939, Daimler was requested to build Shadow No 2 to manufacture 200 Bristol Hercules engines a month. Although such far flung sites as Preston, Lancashire and even Exeter were considered, soon a 62.5 acres site at Allesley, on the north western outskirts of the city, was chosen. On the outbreak of war, in September 1939, Shadow No 2 was nearing completion.

After the war, Daimler reverted to its albeit lack lustre car production and Shadow No 2 soon became surplus to its requirements. Meanwhile at Foleshill, Jaguar was urgently in need of space but was unable to obtain permission to expand. Lyons then thought of Daimler's redundant Shadow. 'After many hours of talks with the "powers that be" [Sir Archibald Rowland, permanent secretary to the Ministry of Supply], I was able to purchase the Browns Lane factory – the only shadow factory, I believe today, not on a rental basis', Lyons was later to recall. By November 1952 Jaguar was established at Allesley, the year-long move being undertaken with no interruption to car output, masterminded by production manager, John Silver. When Jaguar purchased the Daimler company in 1960, it acquired Shadow 1, the two plants once again coming under common direction.

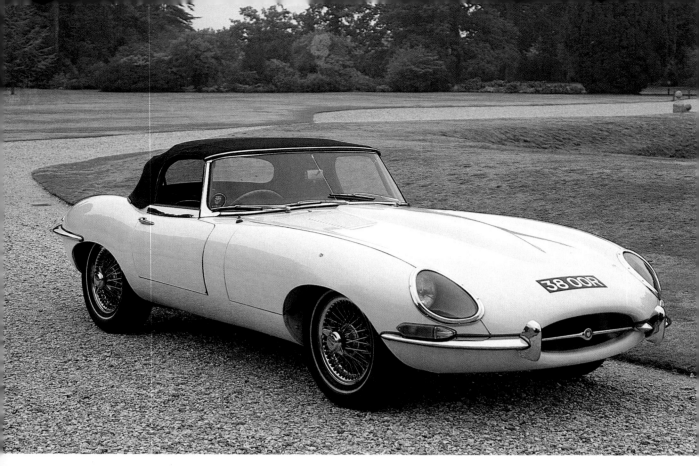

A 1962 Series I 3.8-litre roadster (chassis number 850538), on loan to the National Motor Museum at Beaulieu.

A driver's view from the 3.8's cockpit.

Fixed-head coupe E-type production at Browns Lane in 1967. Right-hand drive cars are shown in the foreground while left-hand drive examples destined for the American market, easily identifiable by their white wall tyres, can be seen in the background.

The 2.4-Litre

In addition to its existing cars, in 1955 the firm introduced a supplementary and highly successful model. This was Jaguar's first unitary construction saloon. The existing Mark VII and XK120 were relatively low production models but the new medium-sized car, powered by a short stroke 2.4-litre version of the XK engine, was the first Jaguar to be produced in anything like quantity, an impressive 92,560 being built over an eighteen-year production span. Enduring until 1968, it had emerged in greatly improved Mark II form in 1960. Over the same period, total Jaguar output rose from 9,900 cars in the 2.4's introductory year, to 24,315 on the Mark II's demise. As Lyons

Jaguar's factory at Browns Lane, Allesley, Coventry, its home since 1952. The upper portion of the large block at the centre of the picture contained No 1 paint shop, alongside which the E-type line was housed for a time.

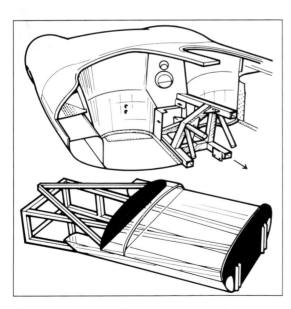

The origins of the E-type's monocoque/ frame construction can be found in the D-type of 1954 though, on production cars, the upper tubular members were angled downwards to give the drivers more elbow room.

later put it: 'This range ... accounted for a substantial increase, not only in our volume of production, but also in our profits which rose five fold between 1955 and 1968.'

Work on the XK150's replacement, destined to be the E-type, did not begin until late in 1956: it says much for the secondary importance that Jaguar gave its sports cars that development was undertaken with a small team and at a relatively slow pace. Corporate resources had been initially concentrated on getting the all-important Mark II saloon into production in 1959 and the E-type did not make its appearance until March 1961: 4½ years after the work had begun.

THE E'S FIRST STEPS: THE PROTOTYPES

In December 1956, operating under the direction of chief engineer William Heynes, Malcolm Sayer began work on the body lines

The 2.4 litre E1A of 1957, which represented the physical start of the E-type project, pictured in 1958 at Christopher Jennings' farm, Gelli-deg, Kidwelly, Carmarthenshire. This is a much smaller car than the production model, also note E1A's extended front sill at the point at which it meets the bonnet, in contrast to the E-type proper.

A 1964 Series I 3.8-litre coupe

of what was to be the first prototype E-type, unofficially designated E1A (standing for E [type] 1 Aluminium) at a formative stage in its creation. The title has subsequently stuck! Aluminium was indeed used extensively for the construction of this car, which was completed by May 1957.

It was relatively small, compared with the production model, though its overall length of 14ft 2in (4.32m) made it larger than the D-type, while its pale green bodywork clearly revealed the shape of things to come. Its under-body structure was essentially a development of the D-type, with a central monocoque tub, while its alloy framework was non-detachable in the manner of the 1954 cars. Under the bonnet, which accordingly did not require a bulge, was a 2.4-litre

XK engine, courtesy of the Mark I saloon. But it was at the rear end that E1A differed radically from its D-type progenitor in that, instead of a live axle, it was fitted with a new independent rear-suspension system. In its formative state the wheel hubs were carried by twin swinging links, while the differential was mounted directly to a steel reinforcement, though, on the debit side, it transmitted noise and vibration to the rest of the car.

E1A was, quite rightly, given a hard time. It was extensively tested at MIRA's Lindley proving ground while lengthy road tests were undertaken, often from Coventry to Wales – a favourite motor industry testing route. The car was usually driven by Jaguar drivers Norman Dewis, Phil Weaver and even William Heynes himself.

Then, in May 1958, came a totally candid and detached appraisal of E1A from a respected independent commentator. At this time Christopher Jennings was editor of *The Motor* weekly magazine, a position he held, with great distinction, from 1948 until 1960. William Heynes was keen for Jennings to evaluate E1A, though Lyons was apprehensive about letting an experimental car outside the factory, despite his regard for Jennings. However, he later agreed to Heynes' initiative. Christopher Jennings owned a farm at Kidwelly, Carmarthenshire and was able to report to the factory of a drive in E1A over the 48.5 miles (78km) South Wales route which he used for evaluating manufacturers' cars. Prior to taking over E1A, the most impressive performance had come from David Brown's Aston Martin with a Le Mans specification engine. As Paul Skilleter reveals in *Jaguar Sports Cars* (Haynes, 1975), in a confidential memorandum to his Temple Press managing director, Jennings wrote: 'The result was almost fantastic.' He had been able to average 67.7mph (108kph), in E1A, which was some seven minutes quicker than the Aston Martin had achieved. With great prescience he opined: 'It will be seen therefore ... that the new Jaguar is a potential world beater' and envisaged the E-type, as it was already known, as having a top speed of '... not very far short of 150mph (241kph), which is going to make us think'.

The 3.8's rear light cluster. This was used on the E-type from 1961 until the arrival of the Series II cars in 1968.

The 1967 'Series I ½' E-type, pictured with its long nose D-type progenitor. In this instance it is the ex-Duncan Hamilton car.

Jaguar by this time had another E-type prototype on the road, which more closely resembled the production model. It had begun life as a steel-bodied shell held together with Pop-Rivets, and served essentially as a mock-up to evaluate the appearance of a full-sized car and as a structure on which to offer up various components. Then Heynes decided that it should be made roadworthy and although most of the Pop-Rivets were carefully removed, this car was always known as the Pop-Rivet Special!

By 1958, the E-type was gradually evolving, and that year a start was made on what was to emerge as the replacement for the Mark VII line (which had developed into the VIII and IX cars): the large Mark X saloon, which was announced in October 1961, eight months after the E-type. In addition to both models, in effect, sharing the same 3.8-litre power unit, even more significantly, a new independent rear-suspension was created for their common use.

E1A had featured a basic independent layout. But early in October 1958 Sir William Lyons was in conversation with Robert (Bob) J Knight, who would later take over as Jaguar's chief engineer on Heynes' retirement in 1969. Knight claimed that he could design and have a new system running within a month. Knight later observed that Lyons would have won either way, whether it was the bet, or a new system for the company. As it happened, Knight produced his concept within twenty-seven days and while a description belongs to the next chapter, it is worth setting down that this highly acclaimed system is still in use on the XJ-S and XJ12, no less than thirty-one years after it was designed.

Jaguar's line-up of post-war sports cars and sports-racers.
From left to right: XK120, 1953 C-type XKC050, ex-Jim Clark
D-type XKD517 and 1967 'Series I½' E-type, one of Jaguar's
hard-working press cars.

Project E2A

By July 1959 there were no less than three E-type prototypes in existence which would pave the way for the car proper in 1961. But there was to be another all-important variation before the E-type made its sensational 1961 debut, and the public would have its clearest pointer to the appearance and specification of the new car at Le Mans in 1960. It was not an E-type prototype, as such, but a sports-racer, created under Heynes' direction, which would have succeeded the D-type had not Jaguar decided to withdraw from racing in 1956.

Coded E2A, the D-type ancestry was all too apparent by the time of completion on 27 February 1960. Work had started on 1 January. Although D-type based, with its monocoque tub and triangulated front section carrying the engine, gearbox and torsion bar front-suspension, there were some important differences to E2A which were pointers to the future. E2A was bigger than its predecessor, with an 8ft (2.44m) wheelbase – the same as for the yet to be announced E-type – rather than the D's 7ft 6in (2.29m) wheelbase. The central tub of E2A was similar, however, to the D's and built entirely of aluminium alloy, riveted together, while the interior panels were drilled for lightness, where appropriate, a concession perhaps to the car's disappointing weight of 19.6cwt (995kg) with a full petrol tank.

E2A differed radically from the D-type in

that, instead of being fitted with a torsion bar sprung live rear axle, it employed a new independent rear-suspension system attached to the main structure by triangulated members, cantilevered back from the strongest part of the central structure. The hypoid bevel differential was attached directly to the monocoque. Drive was conveyed to the light alloy disc wheels by fixed-length, universally-jointed shafts, which also acted as the upper-wishbone arms. The substantial lower-wishbones pivoted at the differential end on a small sub-frame with the other end attached to aluminium housings containing the wheel bearings. There were twin Girling shock absorbers, surrounded by coil springs, mounted either side of each drive shaft, while an anti-roll bar also featured.

But the development of this system had its share of problems. Initially, Jaguar had experimented with a De Dion rear axle, which was duly fitted to a D-type, though this suffered from the rapid destruction of its oil seals as a result of heat building up from the adjacent inboard disc brakes. With the adoption of the new independent wishbone layout the same problem arose, so the discs' temperature was scrupulously monitored. During three successive stops, from 140 to 30mph (225 to 48kph), the temperature of the discs rose to 1,858°F (1,000°C) and the attendant, long-suffering seals to over 652°F (330°C). Two special air ducts were then introduced, which reduced the discs' temperature to about 1,498°F (800°C). These interrupted the otherwise smooth undershield and directed air, drawn from intakes located above each rear wing, on to the forward and exposed sides of the discs. Additional partial air gaps were successfully employed, which reduced the temperature still further, to around 310°F (140°C), while the customary rubber and leather seals were replaced by specially developed silicon ones.

The racing conditions which were to be experienced by E2A demanded the introduc-

tion of a further cooling aid. An oil cooler was positioned in an offside bypass duct and the driver could activate the oil flow by means of an SU pump to bring the temperature of the lubricant down to 202°F (80°C), if severe and sustained braking during a race demanded it. There is little doubt that this overheating problem was one of E2A's two Achilles' heels, (the other was its fragile engine) and one which had not been totally cured by the time that the E-type was launched the following year.

The other major departure from previous practice was the fitment of a special 3-litre version of the XK engine, which is of particular relevance to our story because similar units were to power the competition E-types of 1963. The principal difference between this engine, and those which had powered the D-type, was that the usual cast-iron block and crankcase was replaced by an aluminium one. In 1958 Jaguar had developed an unrelated 2.4-litre-based 2,986cc (83×92mm) unit but E2A's capacity was 2,997cc, with an 85mm bore and 88mm stroke. This demanded the creation of a special crankshaft which, as before, ran in seven main bearings but was secured by ribbed steel caps, each contained by four bolts apiece. Titanium connecting rods, about half the weight of steel ones, were fitted. Almost dry cylinder liners were employed, for although they were siamesed, slots were created for water to circulate around the tops of the bores. The cylinder head studs were rooted in helicoil inserts, in view of the chosen block material.

The customary alloy cylinder head was used of the 35/40 type, so called because the inlet and exhaust valves were respectively placed at 35 and 40 degrees to the vertical. A 10:1 compression ratio was employed while Lucas port-type fuel injection was fitted with slide throttles, as pioneered on the D-type in 1956. The proven rubber and fabric fuel tank, of 26.5 gallons (120.5 litres) capacity, was fitted.

There was a 3.5-gallon (15.9-litre) dry-sump lubrication system, primed by one pressure and two scavenger pumps, with the oil reservoir positioned forward of the bulkhead. All these features combined to produce an engine which was 80lb (36kg) lighter than the customary racing XK engine. A power output of 295bhp at 6,800rpm was claimed though the unit was said to be capable of 7,000rpm.

But the aluminium 3-litre was to prove troublesome. When E2A was first tested at MIRA, on 9 February, there were doubts about its power unit, and it was removed after an experimental five-speed gearbox failed. Another engine was fitted, along with a four-speed all-synchromesh gearbox of the type previously used in the D-type. The replacement engine suffered from a damaged connecting rod and the original unit was replaced. But this subsequently burnt out a piston prior to the race, and yet another engine and gearbox were fitted.

As originally conceived, E2A was fitted with an open two-seater body. The Le Mans regulations demanded a higher windscreen than previously, so that the driver looked through rather than over it. This meant efficient windscreen wipers, and these were mounted at the base of the screen, with a

The E2A, the E-type related sports-racer, pictured on the forecourt of the Jaguar factory, finished in the American white and blue colours, prior to its departure for the 1960 Le Mans 24-hour race. The rear brake cooling duct behind the driver's door can be clearly seen.

Briggs Swift Cunningham (born 1907)

The American Briggs Cunningham is one of Jaguar's most ardent champions, with a two-fold commitment to the E-type: at the Le Mans 24-hour race, and as one of the firm's most important US distributors.

Cunningham was born in Cincinnati, Ohio and his life-long devotion to motor racing was forged at Yale in 1915 when he met Ralph De Palma, who had just won that year's Indianapolis 500-mile race. Thirty-five years later, in 1950, he entered the Le Mans 24-hour race for the first time and was placed eleventh in a Cadillac Special finished in America's distinctive white and blue livery. He drove there again in 1951 with three purpose-built Chrysler-engined Cunninghams but he did not finish, though placed fourth in 1952. He attained his best-ever position (third) in 1953 with other Cunninghams in seventh and tenth places. One of his cars was third in 1954 and Briggs was fifth. However, Cunningham car production ceased in 1955.

Briggs Cunningham entered three Chevrolet Corvettes at Le Mans in 1960, where one came eighth overall and fifth in the GT class. This was the year, it will be recalled, that he also fielded the E-type-based racing prototype E2A though without success. But Briggs' devotion to the E-type was undiminished. He entered, and drove, a factory modified and lightened fixed-head coupe E-type at Le Mans in 1962, and achieved a creditable fourth placing. In 1963 came a team of no less than three lightweight E-types and, although two dropped out, the surviving car attained eighth position, which was Jaguar's last placing at the Sarthe circuit for twenty-two years.

In 1965 Cunningham opened his Motor Museum at Costa Mesa, California where his racing days with Jaguar were reflected by the display of two illustrious E-types: his 1962 Le Mans fixed-head and one of the trio of 1963 lightweights. These were among the eighty-strong collection which was dispersed when Cunningham disposed of the contents of his museum in 1988.

secondary unit located above it and mounted on the metal surround. Blades were specially produced by Trico which was successfully tested at speeds of up to 160mph (257kph).

In February, just as E2A was nearing completion, the company was approached by American racing driver, arch-Jaguar enthusiast and distributor, Briggs Cunningham, who asked whether he could enter one of its cars at that year's Le Mans race. Curiously, the firm later suggested the newly built E2A and, after its numerous engine transplants, it put up a good showing on the 9 April practice day. Subsequently a tail fin was added, which improved the car's directional stability, splitting air flow across the tail

and reducing turbulence, all of which contributed to a further 300rpm being attainable in top gear.

Finished in America's white and blue colours for Le Mans proper, E2A was entered in the prototype class. Driven by Walter Hansgen and Dan Gurney, it put up an unspectacular performance: the race was soon over for the Jaguar when it withdrew on Sunday at 1.40am while in thirty-fourth position. It had dropped out with a burnt-out piston, caused by a fractured injection pipe, which weakened the mixture.

There would be no such mishaps when, nine months later, the E-type proper made its sensational debut at the 1961 Geneva Motor Show.

2 Jubilation in Geneva

'It is not often that I use the word "fabulous" about a car, but the "E" type fully deserves that description.'

Jack Brabham in *Motor Racing*, May 1961

Today it is difficult to imagine the impact the E-type made on its announcement at the 1961 Geneva Show. Here was a race-bred, visually sensational, 150mph (241kph) sports car that was indisputably a Jaguar and, consequently, looked like nothing else.

The new car was slightly shorter, at 14ft 7.3in (4.45m), a good 5cwt (254kg) lighter and, above all, faster than the XK150 it replaced. But in the best Jaguar traditions, it was perhaps the E-type's price which caused the same sensation that had greeted the S.S.1. back in 1931! The open two-seater was priced at £2,097 while the fixed-head coupe was £99 more at £2,196. This made it, in theory at least, the fastest car on the British market with its nearest rival, the Aston Martin DB4, selling for £3,968, or at about twice its price. However, on the all-important American market, the principal competition came from General Motors' newly introduced glassfibre bodied 5.3-litre Chevrolet Corvette, which sold for $4,038 in open form on its home territory, while the equivalent E-type was a good $1,500 more at $5,595.

The E-type's origins were all too obvious to anyone familiar with the D's construction, though the central monocoque was of steel, rather than magnesium alloy and was completely different in detail. The stressed centre shell was built-up almost entirely of 20 gauge sheet steel, produced for Jaguar by Pressed Steel, and welded together. At its forward end the scuttle was strengthened by a horse-shoe-shaped surround with its ends joined to deep, hollow sills. These, in their turn, were attached at their extremities to a strong hollow member, which ran across the car just ahead of the rear-suspension. There was, in addition, a deep transmission tunnel and this, along with a square section transverse member mid-way along the sills' length, formed a link between the scuttle, floor and sills. There were additional top hat sections which were effectively perpetuated on the boot floor, and also provided a mounting for the independent rear-suspension. This extremely rigid structure was further reinforced by the curved body panels. The cockpit area was so strong that it could be retained, without further reinforcement, for the open version of the E-type.

The engine, transmission, front-suspension, steering-rack and big, forward-opening bonnet were carried on a framework of square section Reynolds 541 tubing. The sub-frame proper was made up of three sections: two side assemblies and a front transverse one. The separate structures were welded together but then bolted to form the whole. In turn the sub-frame was bolted to the hull at eight points, with three or four bolts apiece. A lesson learnt from the

The 1962 3.8-litre roadster with the hood raised. Many E-types of the day carried their registration number on the bonnet which was less aerodynamically-instrusive than positioning it below the air intake.

A rear view of the 1962 3.8. The chrome stripping running along the top of the doors was initially peculiar to the open E-type though was also later applied to the 2 + 2 of 1966.

The E-type's unique body structure is clearly shown in this photograph. There is a strong central tub with a triangulated sub-frame to which the engine, gearbox and front-suspension units were attached.

D-type was that this greatly simplified repairs. The bonnet was made in three sections with the joints concealed by a chromium-plated moulding. Although the front-suspension of unequal wishbones and longitudinal torsion bars was similar to that used on the E's XK150 predecessor, in detail it more closely followed that of the D-type. Consequently the bars were mounted in inner extensions rather than in the wishbones' pivots. The bars could bend slightly, as well as twist, the advantage being that they could be removed without disturbing the rest of the layout.

As far as the all-important independent rear-suspension was concerned, it was still a relatively rare facility on British cars of the day. Development work was undertaken on a Mark II saloon which showed a reduction of 190lb (86kg) in unsprung weight, compared with a solid axle. The principal difference from this layout, and that of E2A of the previous year, was that it was embodied within a self-contained fabricated steel bridgepiece which could be removed complete from the car. The Salisbury 4HU hypoid bevel gear incorporated a Powr-Lok limited-slip differential, the casing being rigidly bolted to the top and sides of the bridge.

The Dunlop disc brakes were mounted inboard adjoining the casing while the tubular drive shafts, universally mounted at both ends, also formed the upper-suspension links. No sliding joints were employed. Transverse loading was catered for by the

*The E-type's self-contained independent rear-suspension
system shared, in essence, with the contemporary Mark X and
the later XJ saloons. Note the inboard disc brakes, aluminium
wheel carriers and anti-roll bar.*

use of taper roller bearings at both ends of
the shaft, with the hubs housed in light alloy
castings which also extended downwards to
provide a pivot point for the lower links
below, and parallel with, the half shafts.
These were formed of single tubular members of approximately 2.5in (63mm) external
diameter. An anti-roll bar connected the
two. Each lower link was sprung by twin coil
springs, each containing a Girling telescopic
damper. Twin, rather than single springs
were employed as they took up less space
than a single unit and would not intrude
into the already limited luggage area.

The entire suspension unit was attached
to the body structure by rubber bushes
matched to angularly-placed V-shaped rubber saddles, two at each side, which secured

the suspension unit to the cross member of
the hull. The anti-roll bar mountings and
the longitudinal radius arms were also rubber mounted. Consequently there was no
metal-to-metal contact between the unit and
the body, and the E-type driver was isolated
from high frequency transmissions and road
vibrations. In addition, the rubber mounting
permitted the radius arms to slightly expand and contract along their length. They
also allowed a controlled degree of a rota-
tional movement of the axle casing, in reality a maximum of 5deg under driving torque
and 3deg under braking. This was approximately the same as a cart-sprung live axle
and provided a cushioning effect aimed at
eliminating transmission shudder.

The E-type's engine was the familiar XK

six-cylinder twin overhead camshaft unit of 3,781cc, which had first appeared in the XK150S of 1959 and developed 265bhp at 5,500rpm. Running in seven bearings, the substantial crankshaft was produced either by Smith-Clayton Forge of Lincoln or Scottish Stampings of Ayr. The cast-iron cylinder block was the work of Leyland Motors of Leyland. Leyland Motors had been responsible for it from the engine's 1948 appearance and it thus pre-dates that company's motor industry involvement culminating, in 1968, in its ownership of the British Motor Corporation, which by then included Jaguar. The aluminium cylinder head was also twin-sourced, being produced either by West Yorkshire Foundries of Leeds or William Mills of Wednesbury, Staffordshire. Valves operated at an included angle of 70 degrees in the 'straight port' type of head introduced in 1958. There was a 9:1 compression ratio. Triple SU 2in (50mm) HD8 carburetters were employed, having been evolved by the redoubtable Harry Weslake.

William Heynes was to comment of the layout: 'This system has proved extremely satisfactory both for maximum power and even distribution at low speeds ... care has been taken to make all passages as nearly as possible the same length and, more important, they all have the same flow.' This was also an aid to economic fuel consumption. *The Motor* achieved an average of 19.7mpg (37.1kpl) when it first tested the E-type, and owners found 18mpg (28kpl) not uncommon.

Much was made of the fact at the time that the new Lucas SFP pump was located within the rear-mounted 14-gallon (63.6-litre) petrol tank. The pump was of the constant running type, the idea being to supply fuel at a controlled rate to the carburetters. Any fuel surplus to requirements was by-passed back to the tank. It was so designed to prevent vapour lock problems, the flow not being susceptible to under-bonnet and engine heat, by eliminating vacuum on the

But why *E*-type?

When Jaguar introduced its successor to the XK150 in 1961, it was called the E-type in Europe and the XK-E in America.

But why *E*? To find the reason, we must return to the 1948 Motor Show when Jaguar's new sports car made its sensational debut. It was the first recipient of Jaguar's new 3.4-litre twin overhead camshaft engine and the model's XK120 name echoed, firstly, the designation accorded to its engine and, secondly, reflected its top speed, which was a very impressive figure for the day.

When the firm entered the Le Mans 24-hour race with a purpose-designed sports-racer, the C-type, in 1951, it was designated as the XK120C, the suffix simply standing for Competition. The D-type name had arrived unofficially in the Jaguar competition shop for no other reason that it was the next letter in the alphabet after C! However, the first six 'D' types, chassis numbers 401 to 406, all carried the XKC prefix and the car was originally designated 'XK120C Series IV'.

Harold Hastings, Midlands editor of *The Motor*, claimed to have been the first to refer to the D-type in print. There is no mention of the car by name, however, in his *High Speed Impressions of the New Jaguar*, following a run with Norman Dewis at MIRA in prototype OVC 501 and recounted in *The Motor* of 2 June 1954, though his Le Mans report (16 June) refers to '... three 4.9-litre Ferraris fought it out with three of the new *D-type* [my italics] 3.4-litre Jaguars'. However the rival account in *The Autocar* makes no reference to the designation.

When work began on a road-going version of the D, what else could it be called but the E? One of the earliest references to it came from Malcolm Sayer, whose paperwork refers to the 'E-type Prototype'.

The name survived into production but Jaguar's American subsidiary wanted the new model called the XK-E, to reflect continuity with the earlier XK sports car range and to stress its twin-cam engine. Browns Lane, with some misgivings, agreed.

The decorative bar containing the Jaguar motif ahead of the air intake makes an essential visual contribution to the front of the Series I E-type.

A rear view of the 1962 roadster with distinctive tail pipes.

The hood lowered to reveal the tops of the original bucket seats, which were a major feature of the 3.8-litre cars.

suction side and maintaining a constant pressure in the petrol pipes.

Equally novel was the electrically-operated, energy-saving cooling fan. Also of Lucas manufacture, the 3 GM unit cut in by a thermostatic switch in the header tank which switched on when the water in the 1.37 gallons (6.25 litres) cooling system reached 80°F (27°C) and out when the temperature dropped below 73°F (23°C). The cowled, slender, two-bladed fan ran at around 2,300rpm and consumed 6 to 7 amps. Like the D-type, the header tank was located separately, and behind, the Marston Excelsior cross flow aluminium radiator which permitted a low bonnet line. At the other end of the engine a hydraulically operated 10in (254mm) single plate Borg and Beck clutch was employed. The gearbox was a four-speed Moss unit, with synchromesh on second, third and top gears.

All round disc brakes were fitted, 11in (279mm) diameter at the front and 10in (254mm) at the rear. Twin master cylinders were employed so that, in the event of a hydraulic failure of the front brakes, the rear ones could still be applied and vice versa. This layout was made possible by the use of an American Kelsey Hayes servo, made under licence by Dunlop. It was an unusual system which applied mechanical pressure to the master clyinders, rather than providing the usual in-line boost of the conventional system which had been successfully employed both on the big Mark IX and smaller Mark II models. Centre lock 72 spoke Dunlop wheels with 6.40×15 RS5 cross ply covers from the same manufacturer were fitted, though 6.00×15 front and 6.50×15 rear R5 racing tyres were available, with appropriate wheels, at extra cost.

Both the roadster and coupe were uncompromising two-seaters: there was no provision for carrying children. Luggage space was certainly limited in the shallow boot of the open car though there was considerably more in the coupe, which was sensibly fitted with a rear opening door. The roadster could later be had with a detachable glassfibre hard-top, costing an extra £76, which, conveniently, could be fitted with the hood still in place.

The car was well instrumented with white-figured, black-finished Smiths oil pressure, water temperature, fuel and ammeter. These were all located in a centrally-

---

THE JAGUAR E-TYPE AND ITS CONTEMPORARIES, MARCH 1961

Make/model	Top speed	Price
AC Ace	115mph (185kph)	£2,196
Aston Martin DB4	140mph (225kph)	£3,967
Austin Healey 3000	112mph (180kph)	£1,175
Bristol 406	100mph (225kph)	£4,244
Chevrolet Corvette	140mph (225kph)	£3,896
Daimler SP250	120mph (193kph)	£1,395
Ferrari 250GT Farina coupe	140mph (225kph)	£6,326
Jaguar E-type open two-seater	149mph (239kph)	£2,097
Jaguar E-type fixed-head coupe	150mph (241kph)	£2,196
Lotus Elite	115mph (185kph)	£1,949
Maserati 3500GT	165mph (265kph)	£5,852
MGA open two-seater	101mph (162kph)	£940
Porsche 356 coupe	102mph (164kph)	£2,097
Sunbeam Alpine	95mph (152kph)	£985
Triumph TR3	102mph (164kph)	£991

The famous XK engine was used in the E-type in triple-carburettered 3.8-litre state, as introduced in the XK150S of 1959, and enlarged to 4.2 litres in 1964. It is shown here in competition form on the Browns Lane test-bed during the 1960s. From left to right: Harry Mundy, Walter Hassan, William Heynes and Claude Baily.

mounted, aluminium-finished panel, which was echoed on the handbrake lever shroud. The matching, but larger, rev counter and speedometer were directly in front of the driver. The Coventry Timber Bending Company, whose association with Jaguar went back to its D-type days, was responsible for the wood-rimmed, three-spoked steering-wheel, with the column being adjustable for both rake and reach. Consequently the seats were non-adjustable but trimmed in Connolly hide with the floor being well carpeted. Visibility was good, thanks to thin pillars, while in wet weather the triple-armed, two-speed

windscreen wipers coped with the curvature of the windscreen. Progressively, washers were fitted.

RECEPTION

So much for the car's specifications. But how was the E-type received by the motoring press? At this time in Britain this meant the two influential weeklies, *The Autocar* and *The Motor* and the monthly *Motor Sport*. All had the opportunity to sample the E-type prior to the car's official launch at the Geneva

The 72 spoke Dunlop wheels. This pattern endured until 1967 when they were replaced by a similar but more robust design.

Above: *The 3.8's rear combined rear-light and flasher unit. Although outwardly similar to those fitted to the coupe version, they are not interchangeable because of the different curvature of the bodywork.*

Right: *The 3.8's headlamps cannot be considered a strong point and were greatly improved by the arrival of the sealed-beam units of the 4.2-litre cars.*

Show on Wednesday 15 March 1961, with the weeklies able to take their cars for continental tests. *Motor* put a roadster registered 77 RW – and the second E-type to be built by the production department – through its paces while *Motor Sport* and *The Autocar* had a gun-metal grey left-hand drive fixed-head coupe, registered 9600 HP, which was a pre-production example and, in fact, the second fixed-head coupe prototype to be built. The roadster 'only' managed 149mph (239kph) though the coupe achieved the magic top speed of 150mph (241kph), probably on account of its superior aerodynamics and lack of front bumper overriders! But in reality, these speeds were never attained by the production cars.

In March 1982, twenty-five years afterwards, Maurice Smith, *The Autocar*'s editor from 1955 until 1968, took readers on a rare behind-the-scenes glimpse in an article for that magazine, when he recounted the famous occasion. The car, chassis number 885002, '... chosen for our test was the very well loosened up LHD second prototype coupe... Chosen may not be the right word since Jaguar used to develop on a shoestring and it was the only coupe.' Smith was the first to recognise that to '... achieve 150mph maximum, the 3.8-litre engine had to be a very good one. The necessary power was conjured-up during prolonged work on the test beds, the engine being pulled out and reinstalled more than once.' The figures were achieved on an 8.7-mile (14km) straight and level stretch of pinewood-flanked motorway south east of Antwerp '... which led nowhere and was virtually deserted'. Today it is part of the E39 running from the outskirts of the city to Herentals. Smith also revealed that he '... later happily ran a 3.8 roadster as an everyday car. It went to London four or five times a week, rusted slowly and never, to my knowledge, exceeded 137mph (220kph).'

But now to the test which appeared in *The Autocar* of 24 March 1961, in the week following the car's announcement. Note that the principal complaints of the limitations of the gearbox, high oil consumption, poor seating and indifferent lights were all rectified with the arrival of the 4.2-litre car in 1964. But clearly the magazine was in no doubt about the E-type's 'outstanding feature' which was '... the performance of this car ... best studied by reference to the formidable list of acceleration figures. They are the best so far recorded, in almost any part of the range, in an *Autocar* road test. The normal limit for engine speed of 6,000 rpm was never exceeded during measurement of acceleration.'

| **ROAD TEST** |
| Jaguar E-Type Coupé |
| Reproduced from *Autocar* 24 March 1961 |

For standing start figures the clutch was engaged at about 2,000r.p.m. and gear changes were made at about 5,800r.p.m. In this way a mean of 14.7 seconds was obtained for standing quarter-mile, and as examples, 0–60 m.p.h. took 6.9sec and 0–120 m.p.h. only 25.9sec. Up to 90 m.p.h. all speed increases of 20 m.p.h. were achieved in under 6sec.

Given super premium (100 octane) fuel, there is an exceptional flexibility in top gear. It has smooth pulling power from little more than 10 m.p.h. straight up to 140 m.p.h. and more. Between 50 m.p.h. and 130 m.p.h. in this gear the acceleration is quite breathtaking, and if even more is desired there is third gear, which will pull comfortably from standstill to 116 m.p.h. Where instant tremendous response is desired from walking pace – on leaving an area of heavy traffic, perhaps – there is a much lower second gear which will take the car up to 78 m.p.h.

Bottom gear will be used instinctively by most drivers for moving off from a standstill,

The fixed-head coupe E-type, the fifth coupe to be built, receives plenty of attention on its announcement at the 1961 Geneva Show.

although it is not really required except on a hill, but unless care is taken in selecting when at rest it is easy to slip into reverse – at traffic lights, for example. The gear lever itself is short and well positioned and the box functions smoothly and silently in the three upper ratios. These same ratios, which are rather stiff to select, engage cleanly so long as relatively slow changes are made – the synchromesh being somewhat feeble – although such leisurely changes are scarcely in keep-

ing with the car's character. The only vibration noted at any time was noted on the overrun, and apparently it arose from the transmission.

Contributing considerably to the remarkable acceleration figures is the new independent rear suspension used with a limited-slip differential and inboard disc brakes to give low unsprung weight. Together they give road adhesion, with freedom from wheelspin, of an order seldom experienced before.

This new independent rear suspension, used in conjunction with a front layout of similar geometry to that of the previous D-type, has provided all that a driver could hope for in such a car. There is no harsh movement in any plane and roll is negligible. The ride is relatively soft and even bad Belgium pavé can be taken with no more than a rumble and slight pitching, but for the occupants scarcely a jolt or shake. At all speeds, movement arising from road irregularities is damped out at once, and there is not even a suggestion of the float sometimes experienced with soft suspensions. The exceptional tenacity to the road of this car is one of the factors which will contribute to the confidence of an average driver in using the high end of the car's performance.

Fuel consumption is modest in view of the performance of the car – owing no doubt to a combination of excellent aerodynamic shape, high gearing and fairly low weight (24cwt). The fuel tank holds 14 gallons (64 litres); there is no reserve, but a warning light is provided. Fast road driving returned a journey average of 18.1 m.p.g., and a 137-mile trip in England, using up to 100 m.p.h., gave a 19.5 m.p.g. average. Maximum speed testing raised the consumption to 16.1 m.p.g. and increased the oil temperature and consumption also. This test car, the engine of which had done a great deal of bench and road running, had an abnormally high oil consumption of 650 m.p.g., amounting to about three times that of similar engines previously tested.

What the other drivers would get used to seeing: the rear view of the E-type fixed-head coupe at Geneva in 1961.

Good under-bonnet accessibility made possible by the forward-opening bonnet is one of the E-type's strong points. The inlet side of the 3.8-litre engine with triple HD8 2in (50.8mm) SU carburetters, air box and air cleaner is much in evidence.

At 140 m.p.h., the car seems in one sense to be clinging to the road, so stable is its progress, yet in another sense it feels to be flying over it. Jaguar engineers are to be congratulated on their success in insulating the car from road, suspension and transmission noises which are so often transmitted to the interior of all-independent suspension coupés of this nature.

The rear drive and suspension assembly is carried in a detachable sub-frame, supported on vee rubber mountings in the body frame.

One of the successful compromises in this design is found in the clutch, which is smooth and progressive in take-up, yet bites with the minimum of slip for a rapid getaway.

Shorter pedal travel would be an improvement.

Brakes to Match Speed

The braking system has twin cylinders and slight servo assistance for the four Dunlop discs. Pedal pressures at the lower speeds seem high, and, when cold, the brakes give the impression of being less effective than they are. Yet at very high speeds both check braking and heavy stopping power are excellent. When measuring retardation for various pedal pressures an improvement of about 25 per cent was noted when the brakes were hot, compared with the first recording with cold brakes . . .

The brakes may be applied hard at 120 m.p.h. or even higher speeds and the retardation is then smooth and very powerful, the car remaining under full control without deviation from its heading. Here the balance (including the selection of pad materials) has been struck in favour of high-speed require-

The E-type's XK engine is revealed in its full glory in a way that was never possible with its more enclosed XK Series predecessors.

The exhaust side of the same 3.8 engine. The dynamo was replaced by an alternator with the arrival of the 4.2 in 1964. The heater unit, complete with fan, is in the foreground.

ments, and until a servo can be devised to provide lighter pedal pressures at low speeds, without in any way altering the characteristics above about 80 m.p.h., the present system is perhaps as good a compromise as can be obtained for such a wide speed range.

What of the rack and pinion steering? It is light at all speeds and does not become heavy towards the full locks. With the recommended tyre pressures it is very positive and with pleasant, quick response to guidance or small corrective movements. For normal driving the balance is neutral with a suggestion of understeer. Up to the maximum of 150 m.p.h. the car holds an exact line and the steering wheel can be released momentarily at this speed without qualms.

Dunlop R.5 racing tyres, which are optional extras, were used for 700 miles of our 1,891-mile test, at home and on the Continent, including the maximum speed runs, when the pressure recommendations of 35 p.s.i. front and 40 rear were observed. Using these R.5 tyres, with their flat treads and firm shoulders, the car would ride across the central joints between lanes on the road with the minimum of weaving – a quality found only infrequently. On standard R.S.5s the joints were seldom noticed at all.

For most drivers the limiting factor in speed of cornering of this car will be their own skill. In extreme conditions there is the slight understeer which is desirable and can be amply balanced by the huge accelerative power always available. On greasy surfaces such as are found in towns, a light accelerator foot is essential with such immediate response and with so much power available; otherwise, sideways progress may result. On normal roads in rain the adhesion is excellent with R.S.5s – the standard equipment. If a skid is provoked, the steering permits instant correction.

Those of our drivers who became really familiar with this left-hand-drive E-type test car managed to get comfortable in it, but space is marginal, particularly with regard to leg and arm length. The knees will fit under the steering wheel if it is adjusted to suit them but then the wheel itself is rather too near the driver. We chose the low position for the wheel (which is adjustable for column length and angle) and splayed our knees a little. The pedals are close together, they do not have ideal pad angles, while the brake pedal also has a long travel.

Occupants are Comfortably Seated

Production cars will probably have seats of slightly different pattern from those in the prototype tested. They will be similar, however, in their roll-type cushions and slightly bucketed backs, both of which support the occupants firmly and comfortably. Headroom is greater than might be thought and no criticism is expected on this score. On the passenger's side the toe board needs to be deeper (a small recess in the floor would help) for large feet.

A reasonably deep and amply wide, curved screen gives an uninterrupted forward view. The screen pillars are scarcely noticed and only to rearward is the driver's outlook limited, though not to an important extent. If luggage is to be piled on the deck behind the seats, external mirrors will be needed.

Trouble has been taken to develop a three-blade wiper assembly which, with the aid of two-speed operation, keeps the screen clear in steady rain over nearly all its width up to about 110 m.p.h. The headlamps, buried behind fairings, are powerful and adequate for up to 100 m.p.h. on a motorway at night, but in mist or fog there is a good deal of stray light due to refraction, which proves very trying. An auxilliary lamp could be fitted in the air intake, which, we are told, is of larger area than is needed to keep the engine cool. The attractive steering wheel with light natural wood rim may have to be altered because of the reflections it causes in the windscreen. Otherwise the subdued instrument lighting and absence of small reflections make for restful night driving.

In the interests of standardization and therefore of economy, several interior features and fittings – in particular the recessed central switch panel – are similar to those of the Series II saloons. A speedometer graduated to 160 m.p.h. and a matching r.p.m. indicator, are placed in front of the driver. Ahead of the passenger is a tiny open glove compartment and there is a grab handle across the corner of the panel and screen pillar. Flanking the central panel are a manual choke lever, and twin heater controls. Plenty of heat is provided, but cold air ventilation in hot climates may prove inadequate. It is not comfortable to drive fast with the windows fully open because of draughts, and on this prototype the glasses need more support in their intermediate positions to prevent rattling. The extractor windows behind the doors open on somewhat flimsy catches.

Generally speaking, the interior is very pleasing in its matt black trim – leather at the sides and rear, otherwise carpeting – with contrasting bright metal panels. A good feature is the soft felt design of the sun vizors, which are neat, safe, rattle-free, and may be swung round at right angles to give protection at the side windows. Indicative of the 'gentleman's G.T.' nature of this car is the provision for a radio and speakers.

The roof has a light grey pile cloth lining, over a thin layer of foam rubber, and round the front and top frames of the windows, as well as above the windscreen, are firm, padded safety rolls. Noise and heat insulation are good and no leaks were discovered.

To form a low bulkhead for retaining baggage, the forward part of the luggage floor hinges up and bolts in the vertical position. Beneath this section is a useful trough for stowing books, handbags, gloves etc. Under the back area of this luggage floor are the petrol tank, to the left, with a small hatch giving access to the electrical connections for the new type immersed pump, the fuel gauge, and the spare wheel. Carried in this wheel is one of Jaguar's special, circular fitted tool boxes. The rear door has no external handle: the main catch is released from the interior and the lid springs open on to its safety catch, which is then released from outside.

Access to the whole of the car ahead of the bulkhead is easy when the one-piece nose section of the body is hinged up and forward. It is not difficult to remove this section. It has a central safety catch and is secured by an over-centre fastener at each side.

With the introduction of their long-awaited E-type Grand Touring models, Jaguars make possible a new level of safe, fast driving. The car tested is the first of a new line; no significant extras were fitted to it and there are some 40 more b.h.p. available in highly tuned versions of the 3.8 engine. Critics will find precious little to complain about and competitors will be hard put to match any of the main talking points of performance, handling, ride comfort and price.

ACCELERATION TIMES (mean)
From rest through gears to:

30 m.p.h.	2.8 sec.
40 ,,	4.4 ,,
50 ,,	5.6 ,,
60 ,,	6.9 ,,
70 ,,	8.5 ,,
80 ,,	11.1 ,,
90 ,,	13.2 ,,
100 ,,	16.2 ,,
110 ,,	19.2 ,,
120 ,,	25.9 ,,
130 ,,	33.1 ,,
Standing quarter mile 14.7 sec.	

MAXIMUM SPEEDS ON GEARS
(R.5 tyres)

Gear		m.p.h.	k.p.h.
Top	(mean)	150.4	242.1
	(best)	151.7	244.2
3rd		116	187
2nd		78	125
1st		42	68

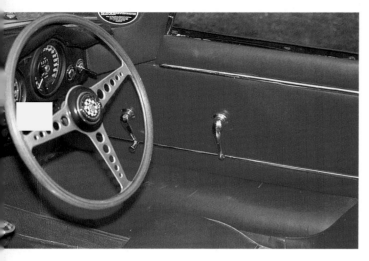

The 3.8-litre's driving compartment. The leather interior adds to the overall feeling of luxury.

The E-type's wood-rimmed steering-wheel is an impressive feature of the Series I and II E-types. Note the aluminium-faced instrument panel of the early 3.8s beyond.

The magnificent lines of the 3.8-litre coupe are revealed in this photograph. It is visually outstanding because it appears as a total entity, rather than as a roadster with a tin top.

The 3.8-litre fixed-head coupe. This is a 1964 example and is outwardly very similar to the Series I 4.2-litre cars.

Sir William Lyons with an E-type roadster. Registered 77 RW,
this car was the second E-type to be built by the production
department and was road-tested by The Motor. *The occasion*
was a rally held at the then Montagu Motor Museum at
Beaulieu in June 1961, to celebrate Jaguar's 30th anniversary.

Because of the shortage of cars, 9600 HP was taken to the Geneva Show where Sir William Lyons, who preferred the coupe's appearance to that of the roadster, was photographed standing proudly alongside it. The venue was the Eaux Vives gardens near Geneva on Wednesday 15 March 1961, the day before the Show opened.

While 9600 HP was available for appraisal on a nearby circuit, another fixed-head coupe, the fifth to be built, formed the centrepiece of the Jaguar stand inside the exhibition hall. There was impressive coverage in the national press and both the British motoring weeklies were in accord that the E-type was the star of the show. The impact of the model

and the buoyancy of the British motor industry, which was the third largest in the world and, in European terms, second only to West Germany in vehicle output, was reflected in *The Autocar*'s Geneva Show report which began: 'Introduction of the new E-type Jaguar – remarkable in performance, appearance and price – and the showing of more makes of car than any other country, allow Great Britian to lay fair claim to pride of place at the 31st Geneva Show.'

Its Temple Press rival was equally enthusiastic. *The Motor*'s technical editor, Joseph Lowry, reported: 'Tucked away in the corner of the exhibition building, which gets more and more vast each year, a solitary E-type

JAGUAR E-TYPE PRODUCTION 1961–1974

Year	Roadster			Fixed-Head Coupe			2 + 2			
	Home	Export	Total	Home	Export	Total	Home	Export	Total	G. Total
3.8-litre										
1961	361	1,368	1,729	134	297	431	–	–	–	2,160
1962	240	2,486	2,726	869	2,671	3,540	–	–	–	6,266
1963	92	1,931	2,023	264	1,778	2,042	–	–	–	4,065
1964	66	1,274	1,340	266	1,362	1,628	–	–	–	2,968
TOTAL	759	7,059	7,818	1,533	6,108	7,641				15,459
4.2-litre										
1964	104	357	461	155	358	513	–	–	–	974
1965	355	1,882	2,237	910	2,146	3,056	1	–	1	5,294
1966	260	2,089	2,349	256	1,648	1,904	612	2,015	2,627	6,880
1967	226	2,274	2,500	205	1,000	1,205	382	902	1,284	4,989
1968	112	1,892	2,004	172	921	1,093	217	1,457	1,674	4,771
TOTAL	1,057	8,494	9,551	1,698	6,073	7,771	1,212	4,374	5,586	22,908
4.2-litre										
1968	125	859	984	147	468	615	146	556	702	2,301
1969	420	3,867	4,287	386	2,011	2,397	499	2,765	3,264	9,948
1970	179	3,191	3,370	412	1,454	1,866	229	1,134	1,363	6,599
1971	–	19	19	–	16	16	–	–	–	35
TOTAL	724	7,936	8,660	945	3,949	4,894	874	4,455	5,329	18,883
5.3-litre										
1970	–	–	–	–	–	–	81	6	87	87
1971	196	144	340	–	–	–	811	2,595	3,406	3,746
1972	445	1,266	1,711	–	–	–	242	1,752	1,994	3,705
1973	909	2,256	3,165	–	–	–	403	1,118	1,521	4,686
1974	175	2,584*	2,759	–	–	–	–	–	–	2,759
TOTAL	1,725	6,250	7,975	–	–	–	1,537	5,471	7,008	14,983
G. TOTAL	4,265	29,739	34,004	4,176	16,130	20,306	3,623	14,300	17,923	72,233

*Includes two V12s exported in 1975

Jaguar coupe is the exhibit which every visitor to the Geneva Motor Show wants to see.' In addition to the car's sensational appearance, Lowry pointed out the highly competitive price which was favourably received: 'Nothing else which is on view can challenge Sir William Lyons' new model at which such refined high performance is being ... regarded with something close to incredulity.'

After this impressive reception, production took a little time to build up. By the end of March, only sixteen cars (ten roadsters and six coupes) had been built. This is probably an appropriate moment to pause and consider just how the E-type was manufactured.

The air intake, bumpers and enclosed headlights were essentially carried over to the 4.2 and would survive as an entity until 1967.

When the 3.8 was introduced, the bonnet louvres were originally made separately though they were soon incorporated into the pressing.

The transparent Triplex
headlamp covers, initiated on
the 3.8, were perpetuated on the
4.2 and survived until the
arrival of the 'Series I½' in
1967.

This design of 72 spoke wire wheels was current from 1961
until 1967.

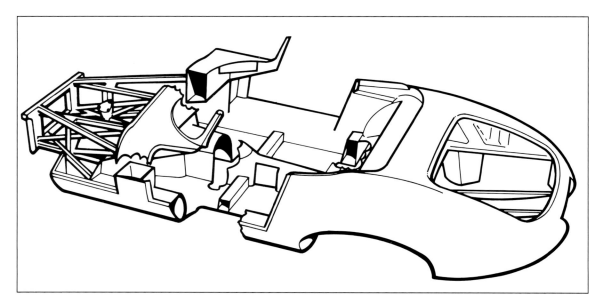

The E-type's construction throughout its production life, showing the unitary hull and front framework.

THE E-TYPE IN THE MAKING

Up until 1959 Jaguar's Browns Lane plant was the firm's only factory but the success, in particular, of the medium-sized saloon range resulted in the works, in Lyons words, '...bursting at the seams'. The Conservative government of the day was directing industry to expand, not in its industrial heartland, but in areas of high unemployment. It was a policy opposed, with some justification, by Lyons but then: 'It came to my knowledge that the Daimler Company, which occupied a very fine site at Radford, within two miles of our existing factory at Browns Lane was up for sale.'

Jaguar bought Daimler in June 1960, paying its BSA parent £3.4 million for what was Britain's oldest marque name. This purchase – Radford embraced approximately one million sq ft (304,800 sq m) – effectively doubled Jaguar's floor space without the firm having to move from outside Coventry. This gave the firm the opportunity to reorgan-

ise its production facilities, and all machining and XK engine manufacture was concentrated at Radford. As a result, Browns Lane became solely concerned with car assembly though the trim shop remained there.

As in the case of the D-type, the E-type was essentially made in two halves: the rear cockpit area and all-important independent rear-suspension, and the triangulated front framework and engine and gearbox. The bodies were assembled on special jigs and Jaguar pioneered the use of carbon dioxide welding for some of this work, which resulted in a cleaner weld than had hitherto been possible. The rear seam, between the bottoms of the rear wings and the rear apron, was covered by slim, shapely bumpers while the front equivalents concealed the joint between the bonnet panels and front apron. In addition, a certain amount of hand-leading was necessary prior to the body being prepared for painting. This particularly applied to the joints between the sills and the rear wing and the bulkhead.

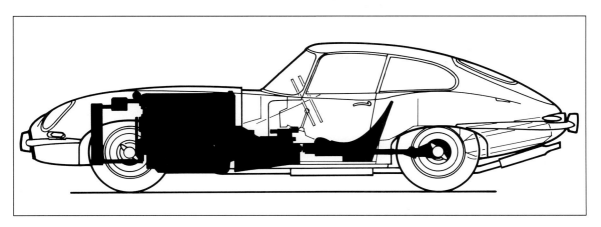

The disposition of the engine/gearbox unit in relation to the coupe body. Note that the steering-wheel is adjustable for reach.

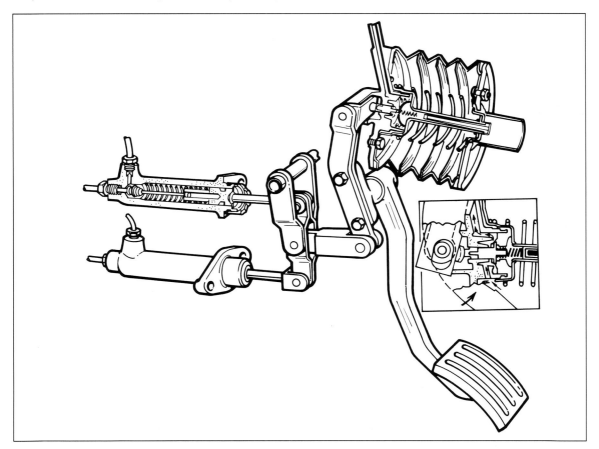

The 3.8 E-type had a unique brake servo, a bellows type Kelsey Hayes system made under licence by Dunlop.

The bonnet is counterbalanced when open and its size
highlights just how much it contributes to the overall length of
the car.

Extended at both ends: the 3.8's bonnet and rear-opening door.

The inlet side of the 3.8 engine. Unlike the later 4.2, which had its inlet manifold as a single casting, the 3.8's are individual to each carburetter.

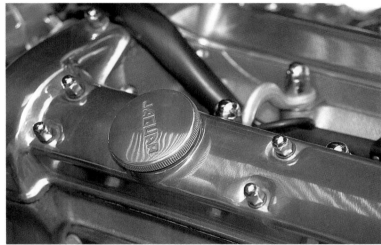

Where the oil goes! The filler cap in the exhaust cambox. Early 3.8s were notorious oil burners though the problem had been resolved by this time. The model has a 15-pint (8.5-litre) sump.

A Lucas electrically-powered windscreen-washer system was a feature of the E-type from the outset.

'The Daimler'

The E-type's six-cylinder XK engine and V12 unit were not assembled at Browns Lane but at Jaguar's Radford factory, still known to older Coventrians as 'The Daimler'.

Daimler, Britain's oldest car maker, began automobile production in 1896 from its 'Motor Mills' in Sandy Lane, Coventry. Such was the demand for its costly, well built products, that in 1908 the company purchased an additional site in the Radford area of the city though, two years later, the firm was bought by armaments manufacturer BSA. During World War I a factory was established at Radford and, during the inter-war years, this plant was expanded. By 1937, the original Sandy Lane factory was vacated and subsequently destroyed during the Coventry blitz. Today a municipal bus depot covers the site.

The Radford plant was expanded when Daimler joined the government's Shadow Factory scheme. This 'Shadow' became operational in 1937, fortuitously as it happened, for seventy per cent of the original Radford works were to be destroyed during the war. Munitions and armoured cars were manufactured during 1939–1945.

BSA had bought Lanchester in 1931 to broaden Daimler's marketing appeal but production ceased in 1956. Daimler car manufacture re-started but its cars were out-dated, over-complicated and manufactured in a bewildering variety of models. These were the years of the vulgar ostentation of the 'Docker Daimlers' but Sir Bernard was ousted from the BSA chairmanship after a boardroom coup in 1956. His place was taken by Jack Sangster, who was subsequently approached by Lyons who had heard Daimler was for sale. Jaguar bought the firm in 1960 and today its name survives as an up-market version of the XJ6 saloon. With the purchase, Jaguar doubled its floor space, while Radford was also only 2 miles (3.2km) from Allesley. Engine production was transferred there, permitting Browns Lane to mainly concentrate on car assembly. Unlike other car makers, which were directed by the government to expand in areas of high unemployment, Jaguar alone was able to grow in its industrial heartland.

In the meantime, the front-suspension, steering-rack and, then, the engine and gearbox were fitted to the triangulated front frame. This unit was then attached to the body assembly on the production line and, finally, it was reunited with its combined bonnet/front wing assembly. Such was the amount of hand finishing which had accompanied the body's construction, that this had to be rejoined to its original hull, otherwise the complete structure would not have properly fitted back together again.

But production only built up relatively slowly. Up until the middle of August 1961, output was almost exclusively concentrated on the roadster, with 372 examples built. Over the same period only eleven fixed-head coupes were produced. From thereon both body styles were regularly manufactured. By the end of the year, a total of 2,160 E-types (1,729 roadsters and 431 fixed-head coupes) had left Browns Lane.

Incredibly this figure was considerably in excess of Jaguar's original estimate for *total* E-type production. It was initially thought that the new sports car would have limited appeal and only sell about 250 examples though this gradually rose to the 1,000 figure. Maybe the relative sales failures of the D-type and XKSS had cast a shadow but, thirteen years previously in 1948, Lyons had apparently been caught out by the success of the XK120 which first appeared with hand-crafted bodywork. Thus the expensive body tooling was not ordered until *after* the model's sensational launch. And so it was with the E-type. In view of the initially low estimate, it only began to rise to 5,000 after the car's tumultuous Geneva reception. Abbey Panels, the Coventry company responsible for producing most of the exterior body panels only created cheap concrete tooling to form the appropriate shapes. It was only when the model was in production and looked like becoming a long-term success, that proper Kirksite metal tooling was laid down.

9600 HP, the second fixed-head coupe built, and the one road-tested by The Autocar. *Front bumper overriders were deleted to help ensure that the magic 150mph (257kph) could become a reality. Alongside the car is 86 year old George Lanchester, Jaguar having become custodians of the Lanchester name through its purchase of Daimler.*

This photograph of a rainy day at Browns Lane was issued to the motoring press in July 1961. It shows fifty-four right-hand drive roadsters being collected by dealers and distributors; the cars would probably be used for demonstration purposes.

The 3.8 engine with lifting lug clearly visible.

The exhaust side of the 3.8 engine. Note that the front sub-frame is correctly painted the same hue as the body colour.

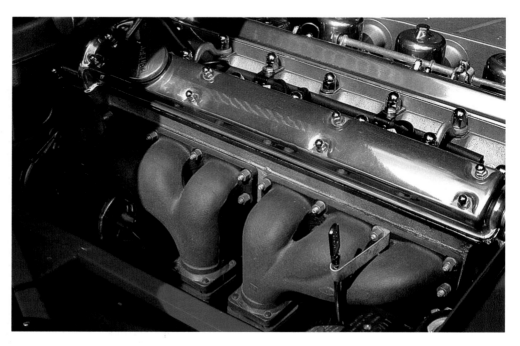

The 3.8-litre's driving compartment viewed through the rear open door. The black-faced instrument panel replaced the original aluminium-finished one when the glove compartment was simultaneously introduced between the seats.

A study in elegance: the Coventry Timber Bending Company's Jaguar associations went back to D-type days and this fine beech veneered steering-wheel was an impressive feature of the E-type from its 1961 inception until the Series II ceased production in 1971.

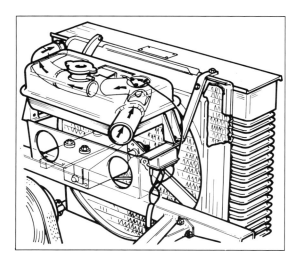

In its original 3.8-litre form, the E-type was cooled by a thermostatically-activated two-bladed fan which, in truth, was not up to the job.

THE E-TYPE IN AMERICA

The model's March debut meant that examples also had to be on show in America for display purposes. Four cars had been dispatched from the factory on 28 February, destined for New York. The E-type was duly launched at the New York Motor Show, which opened on 1 April and was subsequently well received by the American motoring press. *Road and Track* was the first with a full road test and appraisal of the E-type. Even though the magazine had a car for a relatively short time it extolled, with an appropriately Dickensian flourish: 'The car comes up to, and exceeds, our great expectations.' The road-holding, in particular, came in four fulsome praise and '... provided magnificient cornering over

The 3.8-litre E-type roadster was available between 1961 and 1964. It initially sold for £2,098 but a drop in purchase tax, from twenty-five to fifteen per cent in 1962, meant that it cost £1,829, or £269 less, in the final year.

and around twisting mountain roads'. The E-type's steering was considered to be close to the best ever experienced by *Road and Track*. But, on the debit side, there was some concern about the lack of interior space.

This shortcoming was echoed by *Car and Driver*, when it wrote that the car's seats were '... an enigma. Provided that the occupant sat in the recommended position they were very comfortable... However, it's only a matter of time before the squirming set in and we felt our back being drilled by the horizontal bead on the back seat.' The E-type's appetite for oil also alarmed the testers, as their car was consuming a quart of oil every 112 miles (180km) – which echoed *The Autocar*'s experience.

But the American magazine reserved its most stinging criticism for the E-type's gearbox. The ageing Moss unit, which lacked bottom gear synchromesh, dated back to 1948 and the XK120. In an effort to improve quality, Jaguar had taken over its production but it clearly left much to be desired: 'The transmission has such poor synchromesh that gears are never changed needlessly', it revealed. 'We feel that the gearbox is definitely not on a par with the performance of the car as a whole and about the kindest thing we can say for it is that we didn't like it.' The magazine could not see why it was not possible to adapt the D-type's all-synchromesh gearbox as an interim measure until a suitable gearbox was ready.

ROOM FOR IMPROVEMENT

As far as production was concerned, the 150 cars a week mark was passed in March 1962, and by the end of the year, the first full twelve months of production, an impressive 6,266 E-types had been built, with fixed-head coupes out-stripping roadsters and 3,540 closed cars produced compared with 2,726 open ones.

Jaguar Cars, Inc

It should not be forgotten that approximately eighty per cent of the 72,000 or so E-types crossed the Atlantic to be sold in America. One of the most significant and, indeed, underplayed facets of the Jaguar business, was the company's subsidiary there, Jaguar Cars, Inc.

Like most British companies, pre-war Jaguar (or SS as it was) had barely bothered with exports. It was only after the war, with overseas sales geared to steel allocation, that Jaguar successfully invaded the American market. In 1947 the firm appointed Max Hoffman to handle its cars in the Eastern United States and, later, 'Chuck' Hornburg undertook a similar assignment in the West. But in 1952, Joe Eerdmans arrived in America and later directed Jaguar's transatlantic sales, a position he held with distinction until his 1971 retirement.

Lyons had first met Johannes Eerdmans, a Dutchman, by chance during the war, while on holiday with his family at Woolacombe, Devon. The two became friends and Eerdmans subsequently became joint managing director of the De La Rue printing company but left in 1952 and decided to emigrate to America. Lyons read of his impending departure in the *Daily Express*, immediately contacted him and the pair met over tea at the Dorchester. Lyons asked Eerdmans to undertake a fact-finding mission to investigate Jaguar's American sales organisation. As a result the Hoffman arrangement was expensively unscrambled; he had taken on Mercedes-Benz, Jaguar's principal competitor, despite Lyons' wishes, though the Hornburg association was to flourish. Two years later, in 1954, came the creation of Jaguar Cars North American Corporation in Park Avenue, New York just down the road from Hoffman's prestigious showrooms. The firm subsequently evolved into the 32 East 57th Street-based Jaguar Cars Inc.

The arrival of the E-type was timed for both the Geneva Motor Show (March 1961) and the New York Show, which opened on 1 April. There it received a sensational response, mounting a momentum for E-type sales in America which only began to slow in the 1970s.

The driving compartment of the 3.8.

Output dropped slightly in 1963 when 4,065 E-types left Browns Lane. This meant a total of 12,491 cars built in a mere 2½ years, making the E-type the best-ever-selling Jaguar sports car. The previous record of 12,055 cars was held by the XK120 though it took five years to reach this figure.

But outstanding as the E-type was, some of its more obvious failings had become readily apparent. Some were rectified relatively easily. The car's dipsomaniac-like oil consumption was largely resolved from the 1964 model cars by the fitment of new oil control rings and subsequently rubber insert valve guide seals were introduced. American E-type owners also found that their cars had a tendency to overheat, particularly in

One of the 3.8's limiting factors was its Moss gearbox, an 'old warrior' which endured until the arrival of the 4.2 in 1964.

A 1961 left-hand drive roadster is being flown to America.
This is an early car, as indicated by the escutcheon covering
the hole for the keyed bonnet lock. From October 1961, an
internal mechanism was introduced to prevent bonnet shake.

traffic, where higher temperatures exacer-bated the problem. This was often the result of a recalcitrant radiator sensor unit. Owners also found the dynamo was unable to cope with demand, particularly when the car was stuck in traffic. The uncomfortable seats and limitations of the archaic Moss gearbox had also been noted.

Practically all these shortcomings were resolved when Jaguar unveiled its 4.2-litre version of the E-type in London at the 1964 Motor Show.

3 Refinement: from 3.8 to 4.2 Litres

'The Jaguar E-type has been one of the World's outstanding sports cars from the day it was first announced... In its latest form it is very near perfection.'

William Boddy in *Motor Sport*, January 1965

When the E-type's capacity was increased from its original 3.8 to 4.2 litres, the stimulus was, once again, Jaguar's all-important American market. It will be recalled that the E's power unit and independent rear-suspension were essentially courtesy of the Mark X saloon, which appeared at the 1961 Motor Show. Not perhaps one of Sir William Lyons' finest creations, it had the doubtful distinction of being one of the widest cars, at 6ft 4in (1.93m), that Jaguar has ever produced. Nevertheless, it sold better than its Mark IX predecessor, despite initial criticisms of high fuel consumption, poor power steering and inadequate seats. But Jaguar was up against the growing litres of the American V8 which grew untrammelled during the 1960s. So the saloon's capacity was enlarged not, it should be made clear, with a view to upping its 120mph (193kph) top speed but to improve its low speed torque and, consequently, its acceleration. The E-type was to similarly benefit.

When it came to increasing the XK's engine's piston speed, which was 3,500ft per minute, it proved impracticable to enlarge the 106mm stroke without overloading the crankshaft. Instead the bore size was increased from 87 to 92mm. The only way in which the 5mm enlargement could be achieved, while retaining the dimensions of the block, was to siamese all the bores.

Consequently the centres of cylinders two and five remained unchanged but numbers three and four were moved closer together while one and six were relocated slightly outwards. Water circulation was also improved around the top of the bores. As the cylinder head remained the same, the hemispherical combustion chambers slightly overlapped the bores though this did not adversely affect the engine's performance.

Re-positioning the bore centres meant that the crankshaft had to be redesigned and the opportunity was taken to increase the thickness, and thus the strength, of the webs which improved the shaft's torsional stiffness. Considerable advances had been made in bearing materials since the XK engine was designed, those in the 4.2-litre engine were accordingly steel-backed, indium-flashed, copper-lead ones but were narrower than previously. The balance weights were also rearranged to reduce bearing loads. These modifications increased torque by ten per cent while maximum power of 255bhp was attained at 5,400 rather than 5,500 of the 3.8-litre power unit. Although the cylinder head remained unchanged, a new cast-aluminium water-heated inlet manifold was introduced, with an integral balance pipe, with a view to eliminating steam pockets.

There was also an all-important change to one of the engine ancillaries, for the dynamo

This photograph of a 2 + 2 E-type underlines its appeal to the family man and the practicality of the rear-opening door. It arrived in March 1966, had a longer 8ft 9in (2.6m) wheelbase and is easily identifiable by the chrome strips along the tops of the wider doors.

that had hitherto been the norm was replaced by a Lucas 11AC alternator capable of delivering a full charge at only 910rpm, which meant that the battery was being charged while the engine was idling in traffic. The electrical system was accordingly changed to a negative earth one and a pre-engaged starter was also introduced. More powerful sealed beam asymmetric dip headlamps were fitted. Yet another improvement was the replacement of the tank submerged petrol pump by twin SU AUF 301 units. Also out went the original Kelsey Hayes

bellows type vacuum servo to be replaced by a more conventional and 'in-line' Lockheed vacuum booster. It still operated a tandem master cylinder and the separate hydraulic systems were retained.

In addition to this enlarged power unit came a long-awaited all-synchromesh gearbox. This was a conventional unit with cast-iron casing fitted with Warner inertia lock baulk rings which prevented gear engagement before synchronisation was complete. An interesting historical aside is that the individual responsible for the design of this

*Front view of a 1971 4.2-litre Series II fixed-head coupe.
Introduced in 1968, the variant is externally identifiable by its
forward-mounted, exposed headlights, enlarged air intake with
thicker badge bar and larger sidelight/flasher units located
beneath the front bumper.*

Side view of the 1971 Series II coupe, still looking good.

*The 2 + 2 was accordingly available in coupe form only. The
rear seat was only really suitable for children.*

box was William G J Watson, creator of the
short-lived and curious 1947 Invicta Black
Prince (3-litre Meadows twin overhead camshaft engine and Brockhouse torque con-
verter), and of the racing V12 Lagonda of
the 1954–1955 era. Watson subsequently
joined Jaguar.

At the same time as the long-awaited
gearbox arrived, a Laycock Hausserman diaphragm clutch, which required a lighter
pedal pressure than that of the 3.8, replaced
the Borg and Beck unit.

Externally the 4.2-litre E-type – retrospectively titled, like its 3.8 precursor, the
Series I – looked identical to its predecessor.
But internally, there had been a response to
the criticisms of the original seats. Out went
the buckets to be replaced by new pleated
ones, which incorporated modest adjust-
ments for rake. With these, the squabs were
shaped to give more support under the
passenger's knees and a new system for
springing them was introduced. It consisted
of a diaphragm made up of rubber rings
linked with wire clips and padded with foam
rubber.

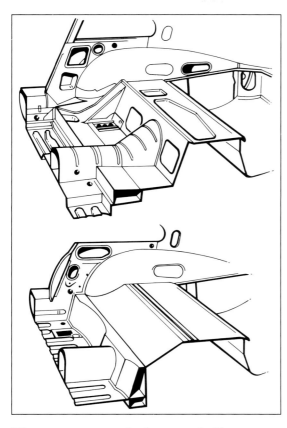

The extra space required to turn the E-type into a 2 + 2 was achieved by relocating the rear box member and redesigning the rear-suspension tunnel, as shown in the upper drawing.

At the same time the aluminium-finished handbrake shroud was replaced by a leather cloth covered arm rest, with a hinged lid, which revealed a useful box for storing odds and ends.

So how were these important modifications received? In its issue of 31 October 1964, *Motor* magazine – it had dropped the definite article earlier in the year – reported on its test of a 4.2-litre coupe, registration number ARW 732B. It was in little doubt that the larger capacity engine and all-synchromesh gearbox had greatly improved the car's refinement.

ROAD TEST
Jaguar E-type 4.2

Reproduced from *Motor*
31 October 1964

The new 4.2-litre supersedes the earlier 3.8 as the fastest car Motor *has tested, with a mean maximum of exactly 150 m.p.h.; this marginal increase (less than 1 m.p.h.) stems from a higher axle ratio rather than more power, which remains at 265 b.h.p. (gross). The 10 per cent increase in capacity is reflected lower down the rev band by a corresponding increase in torque (from 240 to 283 lb. ft.) which, despite the higher gearing and greater weight, gives almost identical acceleration to our previous test car; with the lower (3.31:1) axle used before, there would be an appreciably greater strain on one's neck muscles, which is severe enough now, 100 m.p.h. being reached from a standstill in well under 20 seconds. Using the lowest axle ratio, Americans will benefit from a better low-end performance while British and Continental buyers have improved steady-speed fuel consumption and even more relaxed cruising (100 m.p.h. corresponds to 4,060 r.p.m.) without any sacrifice in speed or acceleration.*

The biggest improvement is the all-new, all-synchromesh gearbox. Gone is the tough, unrefined box that has accumulated a certain notoriety, in favour of one that will undoubtedly establish a correspondingly high reputation: although the lever movement is still quite long, it is fairly light and very quick, the synchromesh being unbeatable without being too obstructive. A good box by any standards and excellent for one that must transmit so much power.

Handling, steering and brakes are of such a high order that sensible drivers will never find the power/weight ratio of 220 b.h.p. per ton an embarrassment: indeed, this is one of those rare high-performance cars in which

*The Series II badge with its thicker
bar ahead of the enlarged air intake.*

every ounce of power can be used on the road.
The new seats are a big improvement but lack
sufficient rake adjustment to make them perfect for all drivers. Nevertheless, 3,000 test
miles (many of them on the Continent)
confirm that this is still one of the world's
outstanding cars, its comfortable ride, low
noise level and good luggage accommodation
being in the best GT tradition.

Performance

Preconceived ideas about speed and safety
are apt to be shattered by E-type performance. True, very few owners will ever see 150
m.p.h. on the speedometer but, as on any
other car, cruising speed and acceleration are
closely related to the maximum and it is these
that lop not just seconds or minutes, but half
hours or more, off journey times. Our drivers
invariably arrived early in the E-type and the
absurd ease with which 100 m.p.h. can be
exceeded on a quarter mile straight never
failed to astonish them: nor did the tremendous punch in second gear which would fling

the car past slower vehicles using gaps that
would be prohibitively small for other traffic.

From a standing start, you can reach the
30 m.p.h. speed limit in under 3 seconds, or
the 40 m.p.h. mark in under 4 seconds, so it
needs a wary eye on the instruments to stay
inside the law. In either case, these speeds
can be doubled in little over twice the times to
whisk the car clear of other traffic at a de-
restriction sign. From 30 m.p.h., it takes a
little under 15 seconds to reach 100 m.p.h.
and there is still another 15 m.p.h. to go
before top must be engaged. Up to 90 m.p.h.
any given speed can be increased by 20 m.p.h.
in 4–5 seconds using third, and in 5–7
seconds using top. Low-speed torque and
flexibility are so good that you can actually
start in top gear, despite a 3.07:1 axle ratio
giving 24.4 m.p.h. per 1,000 r.p.m. Driving
around town, this fascinating tractability
can be fully exploited by starting in first or
second and then dropping into top which,
even below 30 m.p.h. is sufficiently lively to
out-accelerate a lot of cars. Before the plugs

*Spoked wheels were perpetuated on
the Series II E-type but were stronger
than those of their predecessor. They
still retained 72 spokes though with
different lacing and had a new
reworked hub design.*

From this angle, the E-type's body lines clearly betray their D-type ancestry.

were changed half way through our test for a similar set of Champion N5s, prolonged low-speed town work caused misfiring when higher speeds were resumed, but a short burst of high revs in second gear would usually cure this fluffiness.

Motorway cruising speeds are governed by traffic conditions rather than any mechanical limitations; on lightly trafficked roads we completed several relaxed journeys at over 110 m.p.h. on the Italian Autostrada and Belgian Autoroutes. Not unexpectedly, hill climbing is remarkably good, top gear pulling the car up slopes (up to 1 in 5.2) that reduce many another to a second gear crawl. First copes easily with a start on a 1-in-3 hill.

All this performance is accompanied by astonishingly little fuss, the engine remaining smooth and mechanically quiet at all times. The electronic rev counter is an essential instrument, for the human ear could not detect that 5,500 r.p.m. was anywhere near the suggested limit of this magnificent engine. Even 6,100 r.p.m. – corresponding to 150 m.p.h. does not sound unduly strained.

Unlike other Jaguars, the E-type has a hand choke: cold starts are instant after a night out in the open and the engine pulls without hesitation or coughing, though on full choke (which is only needed momentarily) idling speeds are high. The new pre-engaged starter is much smoother and quieter than the old Bendix gear.

Running costs
At first sight, 18.5 m.p.g. sounds heavy but in relation to the performance this is an excellent consumption: many smaller-engined cars with nothing like the same performance can barely match it. Gentle driving will obviously improve the figure but not by any significant amount, as there is less than 4½ m.p.g. difference between the consumptions at a steady 30 m.p.h. and a steady 80 m.p.h. Good aerodynamics, high gearing and an efficient engine account for this unusually flat consumption curve. Only the very best British 100 octane petrol will prevent pinking at low r.p.m.: on the best Belgian, French and Italian brands, it would knock loudly if the throttle was not eased down progressively. At 5s 1d a gallon, fuel bills work out at £13 14s 6d per 1,000 miles at the overall consumption, and £11 8s at the touring consumption of 21.5 m.p.g....

At one time notoriously high oil consumption has been checked by new oil consumption rings to around 400 miles per pint.

Released by two inside catches, the enormous bonnet tilts forward to reveal the whole of the engine and front suspension; an alternator and new induction manifolding are obvious changes. Accessibility for routine maintenance is excellent.

Transmission
With the new gearbox in the 4.2, the slow deliberate change, weak synchromesh and awkward engagement of first are things of the past. Instead, a lightweight lever can now be whisked into any gear as fast as the hand can move, without beating the new inertia-lock baulk-ring synchromesh. First gear still whines but not nearly so loudly and it can now be used to advantage for quick overtaking; the other ratios emit only a faint audible hum. The new Laycock diaphragm clutch is much lighter than before and pedal travel reduced; although the movement is still quite long it is no longer essential to press the pedal to the floorboards when engaging first or changing gear. The clutch bites smoothly when moving off and will accept the brutality of racing changes without slipping and such is the low-speed torque that there is never any need to abuse the clutch for rapid take-offs, quick engagement at 2,000 r.p.m. giving the optimum results. High revs merely produce long black lines on the road, although we were always astonished at just how much power could be turned on without spinning wheels.

Jaguar have reverted to the high 3.07:1 axle ratio as standard equipment for the home and European markets since it gives the fast, relaxed cruising speeds that are legally possible on our motorways, autobahns and autostradas. North American cars, restricted in top-end performance by low speed limits, have a much lower ratio that gives a lower maximum but considerably better acceleration...

Brakes
Retaining the safety of twin master cylinders, the braking system now has a bigger servo which greatly reduces pedal effort. Our first E-type test car needed a 100 lb. push to record 0.96g: 60 lb. is sufficient on the 4.2 for 0.97g. There is also better progression and feel in the pedal, the disconcerting sponginess we recorded at low speeds before being completely absent in the latest car. A slight tendency to pull to one side marred high-speed stability under braking but otherwise the Dunlop discs on all four wheels felt immensely powerful and reassuring.

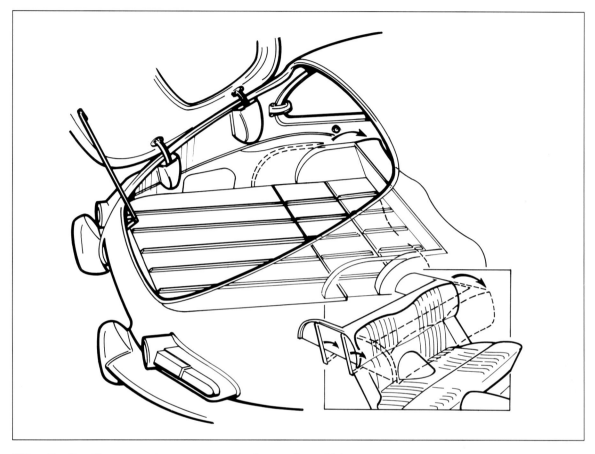

When the 2 + 2's rear seat was not in use, the squab could be folded forward to increase luggage space.

Although a severe Alpine descent made the discs glow bright red, there was always plenty of braking in reserve to stop the car easily without snatch or unevenness, if at rather higher pedal pressures. So long as the brake fluid is in sound condition, and of the right type, heat soak will not boil the hydraulics causing a complete loss of braking. This we confirmed after our standard brake fade test of 20½ stops at one minute intervals from the touring speed – a punishing 90 m.p.h. for the E-type. Pedal pressures increased a mere 10 lb. and pedal pressure was slightly longer towards the end of our test. Otherwise, the brakes were still true and very

powerful – as we expected, for Jaguar's own acceptance test is even more severe than ours at 30 stops from 100 m.p.h., again at one minute intervals ...

Comfort and Control

We found the entirely new bucket seats a big improvement on the old, especially now that deeper foot wells and greater seat movement (two modifications made some time ago) have greatly improved leg room for tall people. A small swivelling distance piece at the base of the folding squab gives two rake positions but most of our drivers would have liked to recline still further: the backrest is rather

The exposed headlights, which arrived with the 'Series I½' of 1967. They were, in addition, moved forward 2.5in (51mm) and were to remain there for the rest of the E-type's life.

upright and tends to support the back at shoulder height rather than at the base of the spine, unless you push back into the soft deep cushions. Even so, the driving position is generally good and one of our testers completed a one-day solo drive from Italy without any aches or discomfort.

An open throttle in the lower gears produces that characteristically hard, healthy snarl, yet cruising at 100 m.p.h. with the windows shut this is a particularly quiet and fussless car, wind and engine roar being unusually subdued. On a hot day sufficient cooling air can be admitted through open side windows which disturb the quietness at speed. Better heat insulation around the gearbox and transmission tunnel have lessened the problem of overheating in the cockpit but some form of cold air ventilation that by-passes the heater would still be a welcome refinement...

New sealed beam lights improve dip and main beam intensity but it is still essential to keep the covers clean, for their acute slope exaggerates any film of bugs and dirt which high-speed motoring inevitably collects. On a very good road, we found the lights just good enough for 100 m.p.h. but generally they are inadequate for fast driving after dark...

Right: *The 1971 E-type all set for the road.*

JAGUAR E-TYPE, 3.8-LITRE, SERIES I AND II (4.2-LITRE) SPECIFICATION

PRODUCTION *1961–1964   1964–1971 (2 + 2, 1966–1971)*
3.8-litre   4.2-litre

ENGINE

Block material	Chrome cast iron	
Head material	Aluminium alloy	
Cylinders	In-line six	
Cooling	Water	
Bore and stroke	87×106m	92.07×106mm
Capacity	3,781cc	4,235cc
Main bearings	7	
Valves	2 per cylinder; dohc	
Compression ratio	9:1 (8:1 optional)	
Carburetters	3 SU HD 8	
Max power (net)	265	265
	@ 5,500rpm	@ 5,400rpm
Max torque	260lb ft	283lb ft
	@ 4,000rpm	@ 4,000rpm

TRANSMISSION

Clutch: Single dry plate by hydraulic operation.
Type: (3.8) Four speedsynchromesh on top three gears.
(4.2) Four speed all-synchromesh. Borg-Warner Model 8 option on 2 + 2.

OVERALL GEAR RATIOS

			Automatic (2 + 2)
Top	3.31	3.07	2.88/5.76
3rd	4.25	3.93	
2nd	6.16	5.71	4.2/8.4
1st	11.18	10.38	6.92/13.84
Reverse	11.18	10.38	5.76/11.52

Final drive Salisbury hypoid, Powr Lok limited-slip differential
3.31 (optional   3.07
2.93, 3.07,
3.54)

SUSPENSION AND STEERING

Front: Independent, double wishbones, with longitudinal torsion bars, telescopic dampers and anti-roll bar.
Rear: Independent, with lower tubular links and fixed length drive shafts for transverse location, longitudinal location by radius arms. Two coils springs and telescopic dampers each side, anti-roll bar.
Steering: Rack and pinion.
Tyres: Dunlop 6.40×15 RS5   Dunlop 6.40×15 RS5
Wheels: Dunlop wire 72 spoke.
Rim Size: 5in.

BRAKES

Type: Dunlop discs front and rear, Dunlop servo assistance. (4.2) Lockheed
servo.
Size: Front 11in; Rear 10in.

DIMENSIONS (in/mm)

Track
  Front: 50/1,270. 2 + 2, 50.25/1,276
  Rear: 50/1,270. 2 + 2, 50.25/1,276

MAXIMUM SPEEDS

Flying kilometre

Mean of four opposite runs	150	m.p.h.
Best one-way time equals	150	”
'Maximile' Speed (Timed quarter mile after 1 mile accelerating from rest)		
Mean of four opposite runs	136.2	”
Best one-way time equals	137	”
Speed in 3rd (at 5,500 r.p.m.)	107	”
Speed in 2nd	78	”
Speed in 1st	51	”

ACCELERATION TIMES

From standstill

0–30 m.p.h.	2.7 sec.
0–40 ,,	3.7 ”
0–50 ,,	4.8 ”
0–60 ,,	7.0 ”
0–70 ,,	8.6 ”
0–80 ,,	11.0 ”
0–90	13.9 ”
0–100	17.2 ”
0–110	21.0 ”
0–120	25.2 ”
0–130	30.5 ”
Standing quarter mile	14.9 ”

The public obviously liked the 4.2 E-type. In 1965, a record 5,294 cars were built and, in March of the following year, came a supplementary and popular variation in the shape of the 2 + 2 though, it has to be said, there was a dilution of those exquisite lines and some falling off in performance. The need for a longer E-type had been in Sir William Lyons' mind since the model's launch in 1961. As the car had been developed from the sports racing D-type it was, almost inevitably, an uncompromising two-seater. Since the model's arrival however, increasing numbers of sports cars were being fitted with occasional rear seats for children, which Jaguar had first embraced back in 1954, when it had introduced them on the XK140. So an experimental car was accord-ingly built and delivered to Lyons' Wappenbury Hall home, which also provided an appropriate 'domestic' background for viewing experimental cars, as opposed to the usually drab factory one. In this instance, the embryo 2 + 2 was subsequently relegated to the stables at the Hall.

VARIATIONS ON THE E THEME

As Philip Porter reveals in his magnificent and monumental *Jaguar E-type: The Definitive History* (Haynes, 1989), in 1963 these thoughts were to fragment into three parts: the 2 + 2 proper, the XJ6 saloon and the XJ-S. Work on the prototype 2 + 2 E-type was undertaken by Bob Blake, who was responsible for the lines of the original coupe. The first prototype was completed by August 1964 and was followed by four experimental cars. The model proper was finally launched in 1966 though it had been intended for the 1965 Motor Show. But *Autocar*, in its issue of 27 August 1965, revealed that: 'It will be a disappointment to many people here and in America to learn that the long-hoped-for expanded E-type exists but its introduction has had to be postponed indefinitely...' Jaguar reluctantly took the decision not to announce the car in October at Earls Court because of the long-term effects which labour troubles have had in delaying production of existing models.'

Structural Modifications

The 2 + 2 was available in coupe form only and the modification meant stretching the car's wheelbase by 9in (228mm) to 8ft 9in (2.67m), which pushed its weight up 1.75cwt (63.5kg) to 27cwt (1,371kg), or about the same as carrying an extra passenger. In addition to the longer wheelbase, the coupe's profile was midly altered. The windscreen was 1.5in (38mm) higher than hitherto. The

There were more radical changes to the rear of the Series II.
The bumper was continuous rather than interrupted, there was
a revised number-plate layout, new light units positioned below
the rear bumper and tail pipes splayed to emerge either side of
the number-plate.

front passenger compartment was, accordingly 0.5in (12mm) higher at 35.5in (901mm) while there was a 33in (838mm) clearance at the back which permitted two children to be carried. The doors were also lengthened, by 8.5in (215mm), to 3ft 5in (1.04m), and Jaguar took the opportunity to introduce 'burst proof' locks. The model was instantly identifiable by a length of brightwork introduced along the sides of the doors.

Mechanical Modifications

The springs and dampers were uprated to cope with the extra weight. Under the bonnet the alternator was fitted with a shield to protect it from heat generated via the header tank and the exhaust manifold. At the same time there was improved protection introduced between the exhaust pipe and the lowered floor.

The opportunity was also taken to offer automatic transmission to the E-type range. Specified with the American market very much in mind, a Borg-Warner Model 8 gearbox was employed with D1 or D2 option. The former position provided the driver with kick-down changes into low or intermediate positions, instead of only the latter when D2 was selected. On the home market this

A close-up of the Series II's redesigned rear lights, as demanded by the American safety regulations.

Rear view of the 2 + 2 through the open tailgate, with the back seat raised, though it folded down to provide additional luggage space when not in use.

meant that the final drive ratio was changed from 3.07:1 of the manual cars to 2.88:1. However, on the American market where top speed played second fiddle to off-the-mark acceleration, a final drive ratio of 3.54:1 was employed.

Cosmetic Modifications

In addition to the seating improvements, other changes included a deep glove compartment, with lockable lid, and a full width parcel shelf below. Instrument lighting was improved and was green-tinted. Heating and de-misting, always a Jaguar weak point, were also changed with variable direction outlet nozzles, as fitted to the contemporary Mark II-derived S-type saloon.

Reactions

So did this extra weight unduly affect the 2 + 2's performance? In its issue of 15 June 1966, *Autocar*, as it had been since 1962, reported on a road test of a 2 + 2 and commented on how little the car's increased weight had affected the E-type's performance:

'Just how much is not easy to determine, as the indirect gearbox ratios have been lowered for better acceleration... This makes the 2 + 2 slightly quicker getting away than the two-seater we tested a year ago, but by 100mph it has lagged behind by just under 2sec. Even so it still makes 100 comfortably under 20sec from rest. From 20 to 8mph in third takes 13.8sec in the 2 + 2 compared with 14.2sec in last year's two-seater, so it is really a case of gaining on the swings and not loosing very much on the roundabouts.'

As far as the improved seating was concerned – 'two children ... tumbled in without a thought' – it was also found that an adult could also be accommodated, provided that he sat sideways. The car in question achieved a top speed of 139mph (224kph).

The arrival of the 2 + 2 helped to push E-type production to record levels in 1966 with 6,880 cars built, the new variant proving the most popular option, with 2,627 produced, as opposed to 1,904 conventional coupes and 2,349 open two-seaters. However, overall output fell back badly in 1967 with 4,989 Es built. Exactly 2,500 were open cars, with production of the closed models almost evenly split between the coupe (1,205) and the 2 + 2 (1,284).

CORPORATE AFFAIRS

Before continuing to chronicle the car's evolution in detail, it is first necessary for us to take a brief look at the changes in Jaguar's corporate status which were taking place at this time. As will already have been apparent, the firm had been built up around Lyons, who was sixty-five in 1966, while many members of his small, hand-picked team of directors were also approaching retiring age. Tragically, his only son John had

The 2 + 2 was also produced in 'Series I½' form. This is a 1968 car.

The glove compartment received a lid, as initially fitted on the 2 + 2.

The arrival of the American safety regulations was responsible for the redesign of the E-type's instrument panel. The original switches were replaced by less obstrusive tumbler units. The ignition key and separate starter button were converted to a single unit. There were also revised heater controls.

The handsome wood-rimmed steering-wheel was continued on the Series II. There were just 2½ turns lock to lock.

Although the triple HD8 SUs were carried over from the 3.8, by this time the manual choke had been converted to a thermostatically-controlled automatic system.

In addition to the changes to the cam boxes, twin electric fans were also introduced on the Series II.

The fluted cam boxes instantly identify this Series II car. An AC Delco paper air-filter was perpetuated.

been killed in France, just prior to the 1955 Le Mans race, when his works Mark VII saloon was involved in a head-on crash with an American army lorry, leaving Lyons without a male heir.

During the 1960s Jaguar had also grown by acquisition. In addition to its purchase of Daimler, Jaguar bought truck manufacturer Guy Motors of Wolverhampton in 1961 and two years later, in 1963, the local Coventry Climax company, which manufactured fire pumps and fork lift trucks. The same year there were talks with Lotus about some sort of alliance and, in April 1963, Lyons reported to his board of his discussions with Colin Chapman. The negotiations dragged on and, in December, Sir William said it would not go ahead because of Lotus' '... rejection of our proposals to which they had previously agreed'. But in the same month Jaguar bought proprietory engine manufacturer Henry Meadows, Guy Motors' next door neighbour.

Meanwhile there had been dialogues with commercial vehicle manufacturers Leyland Motors, which had bought the Standard-Triumph car company in 1961, about a possible get-together. Lyons and Leyland's chairman, Sir Henry Spurrier, were old friends and John Lyons had been a Leyland apprentice. But any thoughts of a liaison in the early 1960s came to nothing because the talks could only have resulted in a take-over of Jaguar and Sir William fiercely guarded his company's independence.

But in 1965 Jaguar's hand was, to some extent, forced when the British Motor Corporation (BMC) purchased Pressed Steel, which manufactured bodywork for the Mark X, Mark II and S-type saloons and, incidentally, the fixed-head E-type's roof section. This meant that Jaguar's body supplier was owned by a rival and the purchase led to overtures to Lyons by BMC's chairman Sir George Harriman.

In the mid-1960s the Corporation was riding high on a wave of technological suc-

E-TYPE JAGUAR, BRITISH SALES, 1965*–1975	
1965	1,327
1966	1,379
1967	1,093
1968	882
1969	991
1970	1,377
1971	791
1972	875
1973	1,337
1974	442
1975	173†
Total	10,667

* 1961–1964 not available
† Includes XJ-S

cess in the shape of its top-selling Austin and Morris front-wheel drive Minis and 1100s, but underpricing, and a lack of forward planning, had seen a steady erosion of corporate profits. Therefore a match with Jaguar made sense because there was very little overlap in the respective companies' products and the Coventry firm had always been profitable. Lyons and Harriman met in private and the merger was announced in July 1966. The resulting firm was known as British Motor Holding (BMH) and the agreement was such that Lyons could continue running Jaguar, just as he had been doing, and with no interference from BMC's Longbridge headquarters.

In 1967 Jaguar made a post-tax profit of £1.1 million but, overall, BMH made a loss of £3.28 million, which paved the way, with governmental encouragement, for its effective take-over by the Leyland Motor Corporation, the latter having by this time added Rover to its corporate orbit. The resulting British Leyland Motor Corporation officially came into existence in May 1968 and, in October of the same year, Jaguar announced its superlative XJ6 saloon, which replaced the Mark II and S-type and the Mark X's 420 derivative. Not only was the XJ6 Sir William Lyons' favourite car but it was also destined to endure for an astonishing eighteen years and carry the Jaguar company over what was destined to be the most traumatic era in its history.

US EMISSIONS LEGISLATION

In 1968 the firm was also having to grapple with the effects of new American safety and emissions legislation which had come into force in the beginning of the year. As will already have been apparent, Jaguar in gene-

ral and the E-type in particular were deeply dependent on transatlantic sales. Therefore when emissions legislation began to apply to American cars from 1963 onwards, it could only be a matter of time before imported cars would have to adapt to increasingly stringent laws. Such modifications first appeared on the E-type from December 1967, the model being subsequently, and unofficially, known as the 'Series I½'.

This legislation, which was to affect every new car sold in America, emanated from the West coast city of Los Angeles. There for many years smog was considered to be little more than a geographical problem. But in 1950, Dr Arlie Haagen-Smit, a respected

The Series II arrived in 1968 and this is a 1970 roadster. The E-type was destined to survive one more year in its XK-engined six-cylinder form.

*An American specification 1968 'Series I½' roadster. This can
be identified by its forward-mounted exposed headlamps,
though it retains the original air intake and sidelights
mounted above the bumper.*

Californian biochemist, established a link
between smog and motor car emissions.
Hydrocarbons and carbon monoxide were
causing the trouble and, in 1961, all Californian cars had to be fitted with a system
which contained crankcase emissions within
the engine, feeding them back through the
carburetter. This was extended to all American cars from 1963 onwards. These developments, as well as structural requirements to
improve a car's behaviour under crash conditions, were highlighted in 1965 by the
publication in America of Ralph Nader's
best-selling book, *Unsafe at Any Speed*,
which reflected the growing public aware-
ness of the subject.

This culminated in the passing of the
Motor Vehicle and Road Traffic Act of 1966.
The new legislation not only related to
American-built cars but also to imported

ones, the manufacturers of which were also
going to have to modify their products as
from 1 September 1967. However, some
ambiguity in drafting the regulations resulted in the foreign car makers taking the
administration to court and some typically
robust oratory on behalf of the British
manufacturers by MG's deputy chief engineer, Roy Brocklehurst, produced a four-
month stay of execution, the new ruling only
becoming effective from 1 January 1968.

Externally at least the 'Series I½' E-type,
which applied to all versions, did not begin
to reflect the £250,000 which the firm had
spent on the modifications demanded by the
new regulations. Perhaps the obvious difference was that by moving the headlamps
forward by 2.5in (63mm), the protective Triplex plastic covers were dispensed with.
However, the original slim bumpers, air

The fluted cam boxes were introduced to all Series II E-types though this is in a 'Series I½' model. The twin Zenith Stromberg carburetters were peculiar to the cars which had to meet the US federal emissions requirements, as was the cross-over manifold.

intake and small sidelights were retained. The hitherto eared hub-caps were replaced by earless ones and cross ply tyres took the place of radial ones. An exterior mirror was added to the driver's door.

These were relatively modest and straightforward changes but more radical modifications were made inside the car. In the driving compartment, the elimination of reflective surfaces was a prime candidate for change though, it should be noted, these and other interior modifications were only applied at this stage to left-hand drive cars; right-hand ones continued much as before. The facia was accordingly completely re-designed. Switches were now of the non-projecting rocker type. There was the addition of a hazard warning light switch. A protective strip was introduced below the switch bank while the windscreen wiper motor was replaced by a unit which would cut out rather than burn out in the event of the blades being immobilised by ice or snow. The heater controls were also changed. Out went the sliding control, with projecting levers replaced by flat-headed ones with pull-push action. There were revised demisting slots.

Some changes had nothing to do with the new regulations – such as the fitment of a transistorised electric clock and battery conditions indicator – but a relocated, redesigned cigar lighter was, and there was a new combined starter and ignition switch which replaced the dated, though distinctive, separate units. New seats with adjustable squabs

were fitted, which employed a positive locking lever. A new safety harness was standardised. The regulations even specified a new type of rear-view mirror with plastic surround, arm and fixing screw designed to break or collapse under a 90lb (40.8kg) force. All these changes were undertaken with relatively little difficulty but when it came to introducing new door locks, more radical surgery was required to the doors and their adjoining rear panels. The American regulations demanded that the locks be of the 'burst proof' type and would not fly open in the event of an accident. Introducing this

Five left-hand drive 'Series I½' E-types of the 1967–1968 era; four fixed-head coupes and one roadster, await shipment to Los Angeles. The XKE designation (as the E-type was known in America) is clearly visible on the left-hand car.

One of the 'Series I½' coupes being loaded aboard ship. Note that both the front and rear of the car were protected by wooden boards during the voyage.

new type of lock required that the door be completely redesigned, while its interior handles were also recessed to prevent them being inadvertently opened. New, more rounded window-winders were also introduced. The E-type's steering gear was already capable of not deflecting by more than the required 5in (127mm) in the event of a 30mph (28kph) crash but a General Motors' Saginaw energy-absorbing steering-column was incorporated.

A considerable amount of time and effort was spent in modifying the XK engine to meet the stringent anti-smog regulations. Jaguar experimented with no less than three systems. Originally it was thought that the answer might be petrol injection, which had been race-proven on the D-type, and a Mark VII saloon was accordingly modified. However, these experiments showed that the system was not particularly efficient where it was most needed: and that was on tick-over (in other words in a traffic queue).

Undoubtedly the problem could have been resolved but, along with other manufac-

*This car is a 1971 British conversion, the work of actor
Richard Essame who obtained a brand new roadster body
from Jaguar and fitted a 320bhp 5.3-litre Chevrolet V8 engine
from a Gordon-Keeble. A four-speed all-synchromesh gearbox
from another burnt-out G-K was employed.*

Glassfibre wheel fairings were introduced to accommodate the 7.5in (190mm) Minilite wheels. There was a distinct lack of boot space in the V8-powered E-type as a 21-gallon (95-litre) petrol tank was fitted. The badge confirms the unconventional power unit.

turers, Jaguar was working against the clock and then looked at an arrangement that the Americans themselves had pioneered: air intake into the exhaust. With this layout, air was injected, via nozzles from an engine-driven pump, to the exit side of the exhaust valves. Introducing what was, in effect, extra oxygen meant that any partially burnt gases were sufficiently oxidised for the combustion process to be completed.

This sounds straightforward enough but problems could occur when the throttle was suddenly closed. The mixture could become temporarily over-rich so instead of igniting in the combustion chambers it would do so in the exhaust manifold, which produced an annoying though harmless explosion which, at its worst, could split the car's silencer. To cope with that particular contingency, a gulp valve was introduced into the system, which injected a calibrated quantity of air into the inlet manifold, triggered by a sudden rise in manifold depression. This ensured that combustion was completed in the cylinder. The problem with this arrangement was that it subjected the exhaust sytem to additional heat, which would then be conveyed to the body – to the ultimate detriment of its occupants. Consequently a more expensive exhaust system would be necessary to ensure a normal working life.

Eventually Jaguar opted for the Zenith Duplex system. This provided two paths

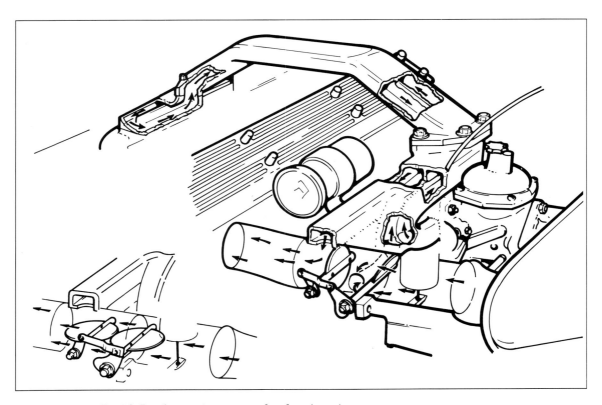

The anti-smog Zenith Duplex equipment, as fitted to American specification E-types from 1967. Note the twin throttle arrangement, shown partially open in the main drawing, to deflect the mixture to the outward passage in the cross-over manifold.

and fabled GTO model. Later in August, Salvadori attained fourth place behind a trio of GTOs, underlining the invincibility of this formidable Ferrari.

Announced by Ferrari at his annual press conference in February 1962, the 3-litre GTO, standing for Gran Turismo Omologato (Italian for Homologation) was effectively a Testarossa with a top, turning the scales at 17.29cwt (878kg), compared with the 22.1cwt (1,122kg) of a typical racing E-type. Although the regulations demanded that 100 cars were to have been built in the previous twelve months, the authorities allowed Ferrari to begin his count with the start of his 250 Series back in 1958. In truth only about thirty-nine GTOs were made. Yet they were virtually supreme in their class and helped Ferrari to secure the Grand Touring Championship in 1962, 1963 and 1964.

In club racing, Peters Lumsden and Sargent actively campaigned their roadster 898 BYR, converted to a coupe with aluminium roof and bonnet, hand-made by Peels of Kingston because Jaguar would not sell them the genuine article. Unfortunately they failed to finish in the Nurburgring 1,000km in May, when a broken wishbone took them out when in seventeenth position, though they achieved a creditable fifth place at Le Mans with their Playford-prepared car fitted with an engine reworked to D-type specifications. They might have done even better and been placed third had not only top gear been usable in the latter stages of the race. Their car came in behind Briggs Cunningham's fixed-head E which he co-drove with Roy Salvadori.

There had been no Jaguars at Le Mans in 1961, for the first time since 1950, but in 1962 there was a Cunningham/Salvadori car, works prepared with aluminium bonnet and dry-sump Weber carburettered engine. As usual it was finished in America's colours of white with a blue stripe. The third E-type was a coupe entered by Maurice Charles

and John Coundley. During practice at the event, it was found that the preparation of this car left something to be desired, so between the end of the sessions and the race proper, it was fitted with a works engine though it dropped out in the fourth hour, suffering from lack of oil. Perhaps inevitably, Ferrari took the first three places, with an experimental 330LM winning, followed by two GTOs. It was Ferrari's sixth win at Sarthe, so beating the records of both Bentley and Jaguar.

And then there were the privateers. One of the foremost exponents of the E-type was Elmer Richard (Dick) Protheroe, a retired RAF officer and garage owner from Husbands Bosworth, who had established a reputation on the circuits at the wheel of a Jaguar XK120 and later XK-engined Tojeiro and HWM cars, prior to buying a fixed-head E-type in September 1961. Protheroe clearly meant business because his E-type's modifications closely followed those of the Coombs car: it had a D-type head, triple carburetters and suspension and brake modifications. Bearing the distinctive and memorable CUT 7 registration number, Protheroe not only achieved a successful 1962 club racing season but was also placed sixth in the TT race, only two slots behind Salvadori in the Coombs car. Another privateer was engineer Ken Baker from Romford, Essex who ran E-type 7 CXW, with aluminium bonnet, doors and boot lid and engine with D-type head. By the end of the 1962 season, he had achieved an impressive twelve firsts and five seconds in twenty club meetings.

THE 'LIGHTWEIGHTS'

So ended the second full season of E-type racing and, at this point, Jaguar decided to take their racing commitment one stage further by developing a special lightweight version of the car, which would be sold to selected customers. An undoubted factor in

Derrick Atherstone White (1929–1970)

This accomplished and dedicated South African chassis engineer was largely responsible for developing the lightweight E-types and is also credited with much of the XJ13 project.

White was born in East London into a family deeply involved in motor racing. Although his father, Bob, was a lawyer he helped to organise the first South African Grand Prix in 1934. After education at Witwatersrand University, Derrick obtained a pilot's licence but was also becoming embroiled in motor cars for, by the time he came to Britain in 1952, he had already built two specials. He arrived as a fully fledged experimental chassis/draughtsman. In his spare time White worked on Kieft and Mezzolitre Formula 500cc and the years of 1954 and 1955 were spent with Connaught.

After Connaught's demise, White returned to South Africa for four years but he came back to Britain in 1959 and joined Jaguar, where he immediately became involved in the development of the production E-type. However, his interest and experience of competition machinery was reflected in his work on the E2A sports-racer of 1960. This led to the chassis engineering of the competition E-types, the so-called 'lightweights'.

Along with Tom Jones, he was instrumental in developing the famed 'Low Drag Coupe' but for all the cars' relative success, this must have been a frustrating time for White, he really should have been at Browns Lane in the Le Mans years of 1951–1956. His hopes must have risen when he was given responsibility for the XJ13, though still under the direction of Chief Engineer Heynes. His ideas for the 13's front-suspension were vetoed by Heynes, who wanted an E-type related layout.

When Jaguar wound down its competition activities, John Coombs' driver, Roy Salvadori, suggested that he join Cooper as chief engineer, which he did in 1964. But Cooper was destined for a sharp decline and White departed in 1967 for Surtees/Honda. In 1969 Derrick returned to Coventry and Triumph but, tragically, died in 1970, aged only forty-one, from a rare brain disease.

this decision was that the newly instituted GT Championship had been won by Ferrari in 1962. In all, just eighteen cars were projected, though only twelve were built. Internally known as the 'Special GT E-type', these cars have subsequently and more conveniently become known as 'lightweights'. The concept has its origins in two cars: the Coombs 4 WPD and a Low Drag Coupe, work on which had begun late in 1961.

The Low Drag Coupe

On 2 January 1962, Derrick White and his associate Tom Jones submitted a proposal for the project to chief engineer William Heynes. It was assumed that the World Manufacturers Championship was to have been for Grand Tourers and the Low Drag Coupe was conceived with that in mind. Although a batch of four cars were proposed, only one (chassis EC 1001) was completed which also reflected the fact that a closed car is aerodynamically superior, and therefore faster, than an open one. (There was a difference between the top speed of the E-type roadster with the hood up and when it was lowered; racing roadsters invariably competed with their hoods raised.)

Malcolm Sayer once again came up with a stylish, purposeful body, clearly related to that of the E- and its D-type predecessor. Sayer's principal considerations were the customary twin objectives of improving aerodynamics and saving weight and the coupe eventually turned the scales at 2,188lb (992kg) which was, interestingly, 213lb (96kg) less than the Cunningham Le Mans coupe, 45lb (20kg) lighter than Coombs' 4 WPD and weighed in at a substantial 400lb (181kg) less than the production E-type coupe. Abbey Panels was responsible for producing the bodywork. Although the car used a light steel monocoque; aluminium doors, bonnet and boot lid featured. The seat was also aluminium framed, and Perspex windows were fitted.

Rear view of the highly-developed Low Drag Coupe. It is shown here after being purchased by Dick Protheroe in 1963 and accordingly bore his distinctive CUT 7 number plate.

The engine was similarly adventurous. It followed on from the 3-litre alloy block used on E2A but echoed the production cars in having a capacity of 3.8 litres. Dry-sump lubrication was employed, with 9.5:1 compression ratio, 35/40 head, 15/32in (635/813mm) camshafts and a lightened flywheel. Fuel injection also featured. A D-type gearbox, complete with a Plessey brake booster, was fitted. The differential casing was also made of aluminium. Once completed, the coupe spent much of its time in the Competition Department though, from the early summer of 1963, it was to enjoy an active competition career.

4 WPD

But what of the lightweight E? The first example, as such, was the Coombs hardworking 4 WPD. It closely followed the layout of the road cars but the principal difference was that, wherever practical, steel parts were replaced by light alloy ones. This meant the monocoque tub and body panels, though steel framework was retained for the mounting of the engine and front-suspension. The latter followed the layout of the original but was stiffer, with production wishbones employed – though with modified mountings. Torsion and anti-roll bars were also strengthened. At the rear, the original lay-

*Graham Hill at the wheel of John Coombs' 4 WPD (S850006),
the first of the 'lightweights'. The occasion was the* Daily
Express *GT race at Silverstone in May 1963. Hill took the
chequered flag, with other 'lightweights' in second (Salvadori)
and third (Protheroe) places.*

out was followed but more robust components from the Mark X saloon, in the manner of 4 WPD, were fitted along with stronger coil springs. Thicker discs were used for the braking system, courtesy of the Mark IX saloon, and the Kelsey-Hayes bellows system of the road cars as replaced by a more conventional in-line unit.

The lightweight theme was perpetuated under the bonnet. Drawing on their experiences with the Low Drag Coupe, Jaguar engineers perpetuated the concept of the alloy cylinder block. The cylinder head followed Le Mans practice, in that it employed big 2/3/32in (51/76/813mm) inlet valves and 1/11/16in (25/280/406mm) exhaust ones and a 15/32in (381/813mm) cam-

shaft, the highest profile used by Jaguar. Lucas fuel injection was employed. A dry-sump lubrication system was adopted to prevent oil surge. This 3.8-litre engine produced 300bhp, a mere 4bhp more than that of 4 WPD though it could be boosted to 340bhp. But the reality was that the aluminium block, based as it was on the original iron one, lacked rigidity and, in long distance races, reliability.

The cars were made available to Jaguar distributors or private competitors with a proven track record. They first came up against the Ferrari opposition in the American Sebring 12 hour race in March 1963. Although the Es proved faster than the Chevrolet Corvettes and had the edge of reliability as far as the Cobras were concerned they were no match for the Ferraris, which took the initial six places. Although the Jaguars were the first British cars home, they only managed seventh and eighth positions, driven respectively by Ed Leslie and Frank Morrill and Walt Hansgen and Bruce McLaren.

British spectators had got their first glimpse of the lightweight when Graham Hill in 4 WPD won the combined Sports and GT prototype race at Snetterton in March, and repeated the feat in the Easter meeting at Goodwood, when Hill led Mike Parkes' Ferrari GTO from start to finish. Roy Salvadori was third in lightweight 86 PJ.

There was further success for the E-type at the *Daily Express* International Trophy race meeting at Silverstone in May when two lightweights once again beat Parkes' Ferrari with Dick Protheroe in what was to be his latest acquisition, the Sayer Low Drag Coupe, which Jaguar had agreed to let go. It was slightly tamer than when originally used by the works, with the original 15/32in (381/813mm) camshafts replaced by 7/16in (178/406mm) ones. The fuel injection was also changed, with butterflies taking the place of the original slide throttles. The Plessey brake pump was dispensed with and a non-servo system instituted.

The first European scrap for the lightweight E-types came at the Nurburgring 1,000km race later in May. Peters Lumsden and Sargent took their new lightweight there and yet another Peter, this time Lindner – Jaguar's Frankfurt distributor – shared the driving with Peter Nocker. Initially, it looked as though the new Jaguars would set the pace, particularly when Lindner led the field on the first lap. But by the 17th, he dropped back into third position and later, while lying fourth, he withdrew with engine trouble. His place was taken, for a time, by the Lumsden/Sargent car though this crashed, fortunately without injury to Lumsden himself. Ferrari was once again triumphant and would have taken all eight places had it not been for a solitary Porsche in fourth position.

Soon afterwards, in June, Protheroe in the Low Drag Coupe, now bearing its new owner's CUT 7 registration number, achieved a second overall placing at the GT class at Reims, held prior to the French Grand Prix. There he was beaten by a prototype Ferrari. The Italian cars were once again in good form for the TT in August. There they took the first two places, but Salvadori came third in lightweight 86 PJ, Sears in another example was fourth with yet another GTO separating him from Protheroe in sixth position. The Jaguars were running for the first time with German five-speed ZF gearboxes.

As ever, the big sports car event of the year was Le Mans. Briggs Cunningham fielded a team of no less than three lightweights, two of which were freshly minted. 'They were', accurately observed *Autocar*, 'obviously semi works sponsored, with works mechanics and Coventry registration numbers'. The trio was to enjoy mixed fortunes. One of the new cars, driven by Walt Hansgen and Augie Pabst, dropped out early on with gearbox trouble, then the lightweight of Paul Richards and Roy Salvadori suffered similar problems but kept going with only its upper ratios usable. The latter was driving when, on the fifth hour while lying 37th, he spun on an oil slick left by McLaren's DB4 GT Aston Martin which had blown up. Heins in a French Alpine lost control and the E-type hit it in a crash which also involved Manzon's Alpine. As luck would have it, Salvadori had not done up his seat-belt and was thrown out of the rear window. He was lucky to get away with little more than bad bruising but the lightweight (S850665) had caught fire and was a write-off and is the only one of the twelve cars to have suffered this fate.

This left the last Cunningham entry,

				THE COMPETITION E-TYPES NOW COLLOQUIALLY KNOWN AS 'LIGHTWEIGHTS'
Delivered	**Chassis No.**	**Engine No.**	**Reg. No.**	**First recipient and history**
1963–1964 15 March	S850006	RA1343–9S	BUY 1 4 WPD	The original lightweight, owned by John Coombs and prepared by the factory. Driven by Hill, Salvadori, Sears, Gurney, MacDowel and Stewart.
4 March	S850659	RA1345–9S	5115 WK*	Briggs Cunningham. Run at 1963 Sebring (8th) and Le Mans (9th). Driven by McLaren, Hansgen, Cunningham and Grossman.
4 March	S850660	RA1344–9S		Kjell Qvale, USA. Run at 1963 Sebring (7th). Driven by Leslie and Morrill.
9 April	S850661	RA1346–9S	86 PJ	C T Atkins. Driven by Salvadori. 1963 TT (3rd).
7 May	S850662	RA1347–9S	4868 WK	Peter Lindner, Germany. Fitted with low drag roof. Lindner killed in it at Montlhéry, 1964 and car subsequently rebuilt.
May	S850663	RA1348–9S	49 FXN	Peters Lumsden and Sargent. New monocoque after 1963 Nurburgring crash. Rebuilt in low drag form to designs of Dr Samir Klat, run at 1964 Le Mans (retired).
June	S850664	RA1349–9S	5114 WK*	Cunningham, run at 1963 Le Mans, driven by Hansgen/Pabst (retired). Displayed at Cunningham Museum.
June	S850665	RA1350–9S	5116 WK	Cunningham, run at 1963 Le Mans. Driven by Salvadori/Richards. Crashed by Salvadori and destroyed by fire. The only lightweight to be written off.
July	S850666	RA1351–9S	YVF 210	Peter Sutcliffe, later Red Rose Racing. Driven by Vincent and Jennings.
October	S850667	RA1353–9S		Bob Jane, Australia, supplied by Jaguar importers, Brysons.
December	S850668	RA1354–9S	2 GXO	Dick Wilkins, who used it as a road car.
31 January	S850669	RA1355–9S	PS 1175	Phil Scragg, who successfully campaigned it in sprints and hill climbs.

* There is some confusion about the identities of these two cars, due to the transposition of registration numbers.

which was driven by Briggs himself and by Bob Grossman. The car was runing well into the morning but whilst in sixth position, a brake pedal pin broke. With no brakes, the E-type passed through straw bales towards the Mulsanne straight though, finally, Grossman got the car back to the pits. There, after some front end surgery, it rejoined the race and went on to achieve a creditable ninth place. It was to be the last Jaguar to finish at Le Mans until an XJR-5 limped across the line in thirteenth position twenty-two years later in 1985.

Mention should also be made of that doughty duo, Peters Lumsden and Sargent, who entered a Lister-Jaguar with a special coupe body designed by aerodynamicist Frank Costin. Unfortunately they had to drop out in the third hour with clutch trouble. Once again Ferrari won the event overall and with the inevitable GTO victorious in the GT class.

At the end of the 1963 season, Derrick White and his team strove to make the Coombs lightweight, 4 WPD, even more competitive. Ever since Jaguar had been working on it, Graham Hill had driven the car at Silverstone and his comments were aimed at getting the E-type to approach GTO standards in terms of response and predictability. This meant fitting even stronger torsion and anti-roll bars to achieve a really hard set-up. As the quotation at the beginning of this chapter indicates, Hill believed that the car was under-developed and was never truly a threat in international competition.

That was the reality, and then a new threat, in addition to the GTO one, manifested itself in the shape of the Anglo-American Cobras developed by Carroll Shelby. Although Ferrari was to retain the GT Championship for 1964, in the following year the title would fall to these Ford V8-engined cars from California.

The lightweight cars continued to be campaigned and put up good showings in club racing though more interesting developments were taking place with two of them in particular: the car campaigned by Peters Lumsden and Sargent and the Lindner lightweight. Both cars followed in the wheel tracks of the Sayer Low Drag Coupe though in the former instance, the modifications were independently carried out with the full knowledge of the factory.

The work was undertaken by Dr Samir Klat of Imperial College, and his assistant Harry Watson, who had become acquainted with Lumsden and Sargent via aerodynamicist Frank Costin. Costin had created the body lines for their Lister-Jaguar, which had run at Le Mans in 1963. Klat had been the first to recognise that, while engine output could only be marginally raised without sacrificing reliability, the way of achieving greater competitiveness would be to improve the lightweight's aerodynamics and suspension.

Playfair Motors of Thornton Heath, south London, who looked after all the cars in the Lumsden/Sargent stable undertook the conversion. During the 1963 season their car, 49 FXN, had been damaged at Reims though it was re-built with a new monocoque at Browns Lane. Beginning at the front of the car, Klat, who readily acknowledged a debt to Costin in this respect, lengthened the front and also reduced the size of the air intake. Although the E-type's windscreen was retained, it was pushed forward towards the edge of the bonnet, so altering the angle. When it came to determining the precise lines of the all-important hard-top to create the most efficient shape, a combination of scientific and empirical principles were adopted. MI drivers might have been bemused to see the Jaguar, sporting a roof covered with a grid and wool tufts attached to it. Manometers to measure air pressures were also attached to the car. It was then viewed and, where the tufts didn't stream correctly, the car was stopped and the offending area clouted with a rubber mallet!

This 'lightweight' (S850661) was delivered to owner Tommy Atkins in April 1963, driven by Roy Salvadori and later owned and raced by Roger Mac and Penny Woodley. The vents in the light alloy hard-top and boot lid were introduced to permit warm air to escape from the cockpit and inboard disc brakes respectively.

All this work was being carried out with Jaguar's knowledge and, maybe prompted by the Lumsden/Sargent initiative, on 17 March 1963, Derrick White and his team began work on modifications to Peter Lindner's car, with the intention of running at the 1964 Le Mans race. Inevitably its lines more closely followed those of the Sayer Low Drag coupe. However, it did have a distinct advantage over that car in that it had the lightweight's aluminium hull. Mechanically, the engine was rebuilt with 15/32in (635/813mm) cams and power was boosted to 344bhp, the highest ever figure attained by a lightweight. Larger wheels, with 7in (177mm) rims at the front and 7.5in (190mm) at the rear were fitted.

Both new coupes were ready for a test session at Le Mans on the weekend of 18–19 April, where they recorded almost identical times, in both instances top speed nudging the 170mph (273kph) mark, behind no less than six prototype Ferraris. Briggs Cunningham had stepped down, so the two coupes were the only Jaguar entries for the Sarthe classic, the cars being driven by Lindner and Ropner and Lumsden and Sargent, all of whom were called Peter!

Clearly there could be no hope of winning the race and when the event started, the Jaguar and independent entries ran fairly close together in 19th and 20th positions respectively. Then at 7.58pm, the Lindner/Nocker car began to suffer from overheating. The other coupe continued to make steady progress and, by the fifth hour, had

This is one of three 'lightweight' E-types, entered by Briggs Cunningham in the 1963 Le Mans race. Malcolm Sayer did not approve of the fly deflector just visible on the bonnet! It was the only one of the trio to survive the event. It would not be until 1985, twenty-two years later, that another Jaguar would complete the race.

worked itself up to 12th place. Then, alas, disaster struck when a gearbox bearing seized and, by 11pm, the car was out of the race. The Jaguar entry continued but eventually dropped out, when in 29th position, the cylinder-head gasket – it had already been replaced once – having blown again, and withdrew at 7.30am on the Sunday morning. Jaguars would not be seen at Le Mans again until 1985.

Later, in July, E-types had better success in the 18 hour race at Reims, where Protheroe and Couldley in the Low Drag Coupe were placed eighth overall and won the GT class. Second class placing went to rising Jaguar driver, Huddersfield textile manufacturer, Peter Sutcliffe, at the wheel of his newly aquired lightweight.

These international events should not overshadow the fact that the lightweights were continuing to prove their worth on home circuits. Jackie Stewart, in 4 WPD, took second place between two Cobras in the Grand Touring race at Brands Hatch held on the occasion of the British Grand Prix in July. There were four lightweights entered for the Tourist Trophy at Goodwood in August. Nocker had been complaining of excessive oversteer and braking problems in the coupe and, in practice, loaned his car to Sutcliffe. Unfortunately he crashed it after hitting a bank at Woodcote though he entered his own lightweight. The remaining E-types were driven by Lumsden and Roger Mac in Roy Salvadori's old car. Both Mac and Sutcliffe retired but Lumsden was placed eighth overall and fifth in the GT class.

Lindner's coupe was rebuilt after the TT in time for him to compete in the 1,000km race at Montlhéry in October. Tragically he was involved in a collision on the 85th lap with Franco Patria's Abarth Simca, after aquaplaning at high speed in front of the pits. Both drivers, and three race marshals, were to lose their lives as a result of the accident. Although Lindner was thrown clear, he later died in hosptial and his badly damaged car was subsequently impounded by the French authorities and relegated to a Montlhéry lock-up pending a law suit that subsequently failed to materialise. This most potent of lightweight E-types has since been rebuilt. The 1,000km ended with the customary Ferrari victory though the GT class was won by Protheroe and Coundley in the Low Drag Coupe, who were also placed seventh overall.

At the end of the year the Jaguar factory involvement with the increasingly uncompetitive lightweights effectively came to an end, symbolised by 4 WPD reverting to John Coombs' control. Later, Derrick White departed for Cooper but then moved on to Surtees' Honda stable, prior to returning to Coventry and what had become British Leyland's Standard Triumph division. In the autumn of 1970, this quiet, talented engineer, who had contributed so much to making the lightweight E-types a success, died from a rare brain disease at the early age of forty-one.

In reality the E-type's continental excursions were over though the car remained competitive for many years in British club events. In 1966 it was Warren Pearce and John Quick who dominated proceedings, along with Keith Holland, who successfully raced his E-type until 1968. Then, in 1966, John Lewis emerged as the rising E-type driver, who succeeded in taking the chequered flag on every circuit in the country, with the exceptions of Cadwell Park and

Lydden Hill. In 1967 came twenty-one victories, while the following year saw Lewis achieve either first or second places – he also won the Freddie Dixon Award for the season's most successful driver in marque racing at selected BARC meetings. But as the decade gave way to the 1970s, the number of E-types on British circuits began to wane, as its weight and the rising cost of competition took their toll.

TRANSATLANTIC RACING

We should not overlook the fact that the E-type was also being campaigned in its largest overseas market, the United States, which began in a small way but was ultimately to be responsible for reviving Jaguar's sports racing activities on an international front. Back in the early 1960s on the West coast, Merle Brennan was by far and away the most successful Jaguar competitor of the 1960s, winning thirty-nine Sports Car Club of America races between 1963 and 1965 having made forty-five starts. Joe Huffaker of Huffaker Engineering, based at San Raeffel, California was responsible for preparing this fixed-head E-type. The model was fielded with equal verve on the East coast and one of the principal exponents was Peter Schmidt, who triumphed in a decade of racing, from 1965 until 1975, and in 1974 won the North American Road Racing Championship.

In the meantime, the six-cylinder E-type had given way to the 5.3-litre V12 Series III model in 1971. But in 1973 had come the oil crisis and in the following year, the showrooms were full of V12 cars awaiting customers, not unexpected in the light of the resulting downturn in the world economy.

By then, the company's American importer, Jaguar Cars Inc, had become the Jaguar Division of British Leyland Motors Inc. Its president was Graham Whitehead and one

Bob Tullius, who spearheaded the revival of Jaguar racing in America in 1974. Tullius' Group 44 organisation, his favourite racing number, was responsible for preparing the V12 Series III roadster for SCCA national races on the East coast.

of his vice-presidents was Mike Dale, a motor racing enthusiast, who had campaigned both Minis and Austin Healey Sprites in American competition. This duo was responsible for cajoling British Leyland, at a very difficult time, to provide support for a programme to race the E-type in America from 1974 in the hope that the resulting publicity would help move those thirsty, unsold V12s. Fortunately they were having to deal with former Jaguar executive and enthusiast Bob Berry at British Leyland International in London. A pivotal factor in the idea being given the green light was that, in view of the backlog of V12s, the car was to be marketed for a further year.

Fortunately for Jaguar two efficient, well organised racing teams existed in America who were ideally qualified to handle the V12.

On the East coast at Falls Church, near Washington DC was Group 44 Inc. Back in 1961 Robert Tullius, a go-ahead Kodak salesman and Triumph TR driver, had succeeded in weedling a brand new TR4 out of the firm's US subsidiary. Tullius teamed up with a good engineer named Brian Fuerstenau, so forming Group 44, which was his usual racing number. Tullius succeeded in winning the Sports Car Club of America Championship for four years in a row and brought professionalism, to what was essentially amateur pastime, and sponsorship in the form of Quaker State Oil. The stable's progress had been keenly watched by Mike Dale, and when British Leyland gave Jaguar the go-ahead, it was Tullius to whom Dale went.

On the East coast Joe Huffaker, who had been associated with E-type racing from the very outset, was approached and he agreed. Although the two firms did maintain a dialogue, the roadsters were essentially developed independently and while the Huffaker team could claim the edge on power – their V12 finally developed 460bhp – the Group 44 entry benefited from better handling and braking.

In the first racing season of 1974, events were soon dominated by two personalities: Tullius himself in the white Group 44 car, who won five races; and Lee Mueller in the Huffaker-prepared silver-finished V12, who was closely behind with four wins. Both drivers participated in the final at Road Atlanta, Georgia in November but Mueller dropped out with a puncture and Tullius was beaten by less than a second by the E-type's traditional American foe: the Chevrolet Corvette.

In 1975, the second year of competition, Tullius and Mueller succeeded in winning ten races between them. At the final the Huffaker car had the misfortune to fracture a differential carrier, which put Mueller out of the race. Tullius went on to secure the Sports Car Club of America (SCCA) National B Production Championship from the inevitable Corvette opposition. This success must have represented some satisfaction to Lord Stokes, who attended the event and had recently been made president of Leyland Cars, its British Leyland predecessor having been nationalised by the British government earlier in the year.

Although the Series III E-type was out of production in 1976, Tullius achieved a further three victories that year and, in August, there was a final farewell party for the model at Laguna Seca, California, when the Monterey Automobile Races staged a 'Tribute to Jaguar' event. Three D-types won the 1948–1956 race though the V12 contest came to nothing when it was Tullius' turn to get a puncture and Mueller had an easy win.

The E-type was followed in America by Group 44 fielding the E-type's XJ-S replacement. These were dark days for Jaguar at home but, in 1980, came a turning point with the arrival of John Egan as chairman. The persistence, in particular, of Mike Dale and Bob Tullius had brought Jaguar back to prominence in American racing and this, in turn, led to the 1982 arrival of the mid-engined V12-powered XJR-5, created by Lee Dykstra whose firm, Special Chassis Inc, was based at Grand Rapids, Michigan. But above all it represented Jaguar's first official, full-blooded racing programme for twenty-five years. The big cat was back!

In Britain it was a commitment which finally culminated in the Tony Southgate designed and the Tom Walkinshaw built and prepared XJR-6 car winning Le Mans in 1988, thirty-one years after the E's D-type progenitor had last taken the chequered flag in the 24-hour classic.

5 Fast but not Furious: the Series III E-type

'I had always liked the song of twelve cylinders.'
Enzo Ferrari in *The Enzo Ferrari Memoirs*

The Series III V12-engined E-type appeared in 1971 to meet two basic requirements: to prove the reliability of the new 5.3-litre power unit, prior to its fitment in the XJ12 saloon, and to prolong the life of a, by then, ageing sports car. Eventually a total of 14,983 examples of the V12-powered E-type would be built, which was about the same number as the original 3.8-litre cars, before the model ceased production in 1974.

WORK BEGINS ON THE V12

Like the E-type itself, the origins of Jaguar's V12 engine are rooted in the 1950s. However, its concept was diametrically opposed to that of the XK engine. Whereas the redoubtable six was conceived to power a saloon with a competition application as a secondary consideration, the V12 was designed essentially as a racing unit and then refined and simplified for road use. A V12 layout had been one of the options briefly considered when what was to become the XK engine was conceived during the war. Subsequently Jaguar engineer Tom Jones began the first brief drawings as early as 1951 though it was not until 1955 that work started in earnest on the project.

Although that year Jaguar had just won Le Mans for the third time, chief engineer Heynes was the first to recognise that, for competition purposes, the days of the six-cylinder XK engine were clearly numbered. One of the limiting factors of the six was that it had been designed during the war when a car's road fund licence was payable on the RAC rating of its engine, and accordingly, the bore size of its cylinders. As it happened the reviled 'horsepower tax' was repealed and replaced by a flat rate from 1948.

Despite its abolition, the tax cast a long shadow and tended to distort engine configurations of British cars of the immediate post-war years when small bore/long stroke power units proliferated. In Jaguar's case, the XK six had an 83×106mm bore and stroke. This resulted in a piston speed of 3,820ft per minute at 5,500rpm. In the words of Walter Hassan, one of the architects of the XK unit and who was to subsequently play a key role in the creation of the V12 used in the E-type, this figure '... was well within the requirements of that time. However, as time passed and racing took on a greater significance in Jaguar's programme, crankshaft speed became a limiting factor in the engine's performance, making a new design necessary.'

'Lofty' England, who joined Jaguar as service manager in 1946 and succeeded Sir William Lyons as chairman and chief executive on the latter's retirement in 1972. England held the post until 1974.

Working under the direction of Heynes, Claude Baily, another member of the original XK trio, was responsible for the layout of the V12. It was clearly inspired by the success that Ferrari had made of the configuration. For just as William Lyons had produced a revolutionary power unit in the shape of the twin overhead camshaft XK engine in 1948, so from the previous year Enzo Ferrari had been unique amongst racing car constructors in perpetuating the V12 unit so successfully employed by Mercedes-Benz and Auto Union racing cars in the immediate pre-war years. In order to meet the requirements of the prototype class in racing, Jaguar opted for a 5-litre engine, and according to Hassan: 'In order to provide the maximum potential in power, a 12-cylinder "Vee" configuration with a short stroke of 70mm was conceived to provide safe running at 8,000/8,500rpm.'

The 4,994cc oversquare 87mm bore, 60 degree V12 that resulted was effectively two 2.5-litre XK engines, accordingly with twin overhead camshafts per cylinder bank, mounted on an aluminium block/crankcase unit. However, when Jaguar announced its withdrawal from racing in 1956, the V12 project was shelved. Then, in the early 1960s, interest in the 24-hour classic was revived and there were thoughts, once again, of competing at the Sarthe circuit.

The V12 ran for the first time in August 1964 when it developed 502bhp at 7,600rpm and the original idea was to enter at the 1965 Le Mans event though, in reality, work on a suitable car did not begin until that June. Derrick White, who had put in so much work on the development of the lightweight E-types, was responsible for the design of the car which, somewhat ominously, was titled XJ13, while Malcolm Sayer was responsible for the bodywork.

THE XJ13

Formula 1 racing cars had become almost exclusively mid-engined from the 1961 season onwards and sports-racers had followed suit, noticeably on the Ford GT40 of 1964. It was to eventually break the Ferrari dominance of Le Mans by winning the event on no less than four occasions, from 1966 until 1969, and it is no surprise to find that White opted for this configuration, with the V12 unit mounted longitudinally behind the driver. A German ZF five-speed gearbox was fitted, the equivalent British-built Hewland unit only just having begun to prove its worth.

The body, of monocoque construction, was made of 18 gauge aluminum alloy sheeting. There was a double bulkhead at the front attached to two broad, deep sills; one carrying two of the car's three flexible petrol tanks (the other was located in a boxed member below and behind the driver) and the other carrying the oil reservoir for the dry-sump engine. There was a stressed floor, and a second single bulkhead behind the driving compartment to which the V12 engine was attached. Suspension was all independent and related to that of the E-type,

Frank Raymond Wilton (Lofty) England (born 1911)

'Lofty' England, who took over as Jaguar's chief executive from Sir William Lyons in 1972, had to make the inevitable decision that the E-type cease production in 1974.

Born in Finchley England was educated at the local Christ College and served his engineering apprenticeship, from 1927 until 1932, at Daimler's Hendon depot. A great motoring racing enthusiast, England became mechanic to Sir Henry Birkin and later served Whitney Straight in a similar capacity. He subsequently joined ERA and also maintained these British single-seaters for two celebrated racing drivers of the 1930s: Richard Seaman and 'B Bira', the Siamese Prince Birabongse Bhanuban.

In 1938, England moved to Coventry to join Alvis as a service engineer and later became service department superintendant. After war service as a pilot in the RAF during the war, where he regularly piloted Lancaster bombers on daylight bombing raids, he returned to Alvis. Through a long standing friendship with Wally Hassan, cemented during Brooklands days, he heard of a job at Jaguar, joined as service manager in 1946 and was promoted to service director ten years later. These were the famous Le Mans years for Jaguar and the lanky figure of 'Lofty' England can be seen in many an historic racing photograph when, from 1951, he acted as its celebrated racing manager.

In 1961 England was promoted to assistant managing director, became deputy managing director in 1966 and, from the following year, shared the firm's joint managing directorship. When Sir William Lyons stepped down in his seventieth year, in March 1972, 'Lofty' England became Jaguar's chief executive though this could only be an interim appointment, for he was sixty at the time. Since 1968 Jaguar had been part of British Leyland and, in the autumn of 1973, Lord Stokes appointed thirty-four year old Geofferey Robinson as managing director. England retired in 1974 but not before he had ordered that the ageing E-type cease production at the end of the year. Robinson resigned after the publication of the government's ill-fated Ryder Report in 1975.

A Series III E-type of 1974. This is one of the last fifty black-finished V12 roadsters made. Its chassis number is IS 2858.

As originally conceived, Jaguar's V12 engine had twin overhead camshafts per cylinder bank. This 4.9-litre 60deg V12 has been prepared for display purposes and appears to be singularly tidy because it has yet to be fitted with its carburetters.

with forged wishbones at the front – though coil springs and dampers took the place of longitudinal torsion bars. At the rear, there were also E-type associations, with fixed length driveshafts forming the top wishbones but with single rather than double spring/dampers, lower A members and twin tubular trailing links on either side. Brakes were all round Dunlop discs, later changed to Girling ventilated ones, though, unlike the E-type with its inboard rear ones, on

the XJ13 they were mounted outboard. When Derrick White departed for Cooper in 1965, his job was taken over by Mike Kimberley. The latter had joined Jaguar as an apprentice and subsequently left for Lotus in 1969. Today he is the firm's chief executive.

The XJ13 was completed in March 1966 though the car did not run at Le Mans in June and, in the following month, came news that Jaguar was to merge with the

The 5.3-litre V12 engine, as it appeared in the Series III E-type in 1971. The single overhead camshafts are readily apparent as are the long inlet manifolds. The wishbone and torsion bar independent front-suspension and rack and pinion steering can also be seen.

British Motor Corporation. As for the car, it was not tested until March of the following year, when it lapped MIRA's banked test track at Lindley, Warwickshire at 161mph (259kph) and achieved 175mph (282kph) down the straights, which suggests that the reality was that the XJ13 did not come up to expectation as far as its top speed was concerned.

This performance was later confirmed by subversive runs at Silverstone, secrecy being essential as news of what would inevitably been interpreted as a V12 E-type could have resulted in a dramatic falling off in sales of the six-cylinder model. But, in August 1967, it was decided to sideline the project.

The reality was that by then the car was no longer competitive. This was confirmed in 1973 by F R W 'Lofty' England, Jaguar's former competition manager, who had taken over from Sir William Lyons as chief executive on the latter's retirement in the previous year. England told *Autocar*: 'By this time [1967] it was about two years out of date, the modern trend of doubling the width of the tyres had come in, and to have got anywhere with it, we would have had to do a lot of re-designing and re-building. Quite frankly, we did not have the time or the people to go into all that, and so we put it on one side.' The XJ13 was thereafter relegated to a corner of the Jaguar experimental department though, as will become apparent, this was far from the end of the story.

NEW DIRECTIONS FOR THE V12

In the meantime, two outstanding engineers had joined the Jaguar company. As mentioned in Chapter 3, in 1963 the firm had taken over Coventry Climax Engines, which specialised in the manufacture of stationary engines, fork lift trucks and fire pumps. It was this purchase which had brought Walter Hassan back into the corporate fold. Hassan, who had worked for both Bentley and ERA in pre-war days, had joined Jaguar from the Bristol Aeroplane Company during the Second World War. He remained there until 1950, when he moved to Coventry Climax as chief engineer. There, with Harry Mundy, he was responsible for the design of an impressive line of single overhead camshaft fire pump engines, which, from 1954, evolved into a series of competition units. Those above all powered the Coopers and Lotus which won the Constructors' Cup on no less than four occasions. There were those who quipped that Lyons had bought Coventry Climax to once again secure Hassan's services!

In the following year of 1964, Harry Mundy, an old friend and collaborator of Hassan's, who had been technical editor of *Autocar*, became Jaguar's chief development engineer. Another ERA veteran, Mundy had worked for BRM, where he had been head of the design office prior to joining Coventry Climax as chief designer in 1950. It was these two distinguished engineers who would ultimately be responsible for making the V12 engine a production reality.

By this time Jaguar had thoughts of developing two versions of its V12. The four cam unit, as used in the XJ13, might have powered a production sports car, plus a cheaper variant with single rather than twin cams. The firm had decided that a new saloon, coded XJ4, then under development and which emerged as the superlative XJ6 in 1968, was to be offered in V12-engined

The Coventry Climax connection

With former Jaguar development engineer, Walter Hassan, established at Coventry Climax from 1950–1966, some aspects of the XK engine were reflected in the firm's racing units, and, conversely, Hassan's researches at Widdrington Road, strongly influenced the design of the Jaguar V12 engine.

The firm's origins date back to 1903 when H Pelham Lee, who had moved to Coventry to join Daimler as an 'improver', first built a car, the Lee-Stroyer, but soon switched to producing proprietory Coventry Simplex engines. In 1917, Lee changed the firm's name to Coventry Climax. In 1937, it diversified into the production of fire pumps which were greatly in demand during World War II. The arrival in 1950 of Walter Hassan and Harry Mundy resulted in the appearance, in April 1951, of the advanced 1,022cc FW (for Featherweight) aluminium fire pump engine. Hassan's involvement in the creation of the XK Jaguar engine was reflected in its use of an overhead camshaft, as was its employment of a similar method of achieving the valve clearances by tappet cups and shims, an arrangement used on all the FW's racing derivatives.

When Hassan moved to Browns Lane in 1966 to work, with Mundy, on the V12 Jaguar engine, the former drew on his experiences at Coventry Climax, by advocating a combustion chamber in piston layout with a completely flat cylinder head. It was a layout that had been successfully used by Rover (1963) and Ford (1965). A FWM 750cc engine, a derivative of the original FW unit, had been converted to diesel operation.

Testing showed that a petrol engine performed better with a flat, rather than wedge head, and, with a given fuel consumption, would accept a compression ratio of one number higher and also developed slightly more power. On the debit side was a heavier piston, though the flat deck head was cheaper to manufacture than the customary combustion chamber-in-head variety. It was successfully tested on the V12 and introduced in the Series III E-type in 1971.

The rear of the Series III model was essentially similar to that of the Series II's though the car was 2.5in (63.5mm) wider.

form as well as with the customary six-cylinder power unit.

Once again it was the demands of Jaguar's all-important American market that dictated the V12's configuration, which in that country between the wars had been employed to power such illustrious makes as Packard, Lincoln and, above all, Cadillac. After the success of Jaguar's innovative twin overhead camshaft six-cylinder XK engine perhaps the next logical stage was a V8, but this was the transatlantic norm. So Jaguar opted for the smoothness and refinement of 12 cylinders, to which was coupled the allure of the configuration which had been greatly enhanced by Ferrari, a mystique which would also be underlined by the arrival of

the new Lamborghini marque in 1963. By 1965 the 5-litre four camshaft Jaguar V12 was already being tested under the bonnets of a quartet of Mark X saloons.

But the reality was that the performance of the four cam V12, in Hassan's opinion, left something to be desired. For although this 5-litre unit developed 500bhp, this accounted for no less than 100bhp per litre. When he had been at Coventry Climax, Hassan had been accustomed to an output of at least 120bhp per litre, which would have resulted in a V12 of at least 600bhp. As Hassan recounts in his autobiography: 'There were, in addition, other puzzles. Not only was there a lack of top end power, there was also a lack of low speed and mid-range torque.'

For Hassan there were echoes of the V12 Lagonda engine of the 1930s '... which looked and sounded splendid, but it suffered from the same characteristics as this Jaguar'. But by the time that Hassan became involved with the V12, the concept of the sports version had been down-graded so the requirement of top end power became less, to be replaced by the need for plenty of low- and mid-range torque. It thus became essential for the noisy, peaky racing engine to become a smoothly refined unit.

One of the reasons for the shortcomings of the four cam V12, Hassan believed, was its inlet ports. Because there was very little room between the V of the 60 degree twelve, Heynes and Baily had opted for vertical

Walter (Wally) Hassan who, with Harry Mundy, saw the V12 Jaguar engine into production. Hassan was a formidable advocate of the 'flat head' single, as opposed to the twin cam head, which was the layout subsequently adopted.

Walter (Wally) Thomas Frederick Hassan (born 1905)

Wally Hassan is one of Britain's outstanding automobile engineers, whose distinguished career included no less than three spells with Jaguar. The most significant periods were between 1943 and 1950 when he played a key role in the creation of the firm's famous XK engine, and the 1965–1972 era, when with Harry Mundy, they made the firm's V12 engine, first used in the E-type, a production reality.

London-born Hassan was educated at what he described as, 'a succession of schools', and received his technical education at the Northern Polytechnic in Lower Holloway and the Hackney Institute of Engineering. In 1920 Hassan joined Bentley Motors and his career with the firm lasted until the Rolls-Royce takeover of 1931. Between then and 1936, he worked for Bentley's former chairman, Woolf Barnato, and his name will forever be associated with that celebrated Brooklands car, the Barnato-Hassan Special of 1934. Hassan then moved to the newly established ERA concern at Bourne, Lincolnshire and, after two years in the experimental and racing department, he returned to his beloved Brooklands and Thomson and Taylor, where he supervised the supply of components for the creation of John Cobb's land speed record Napier Railton of 1938.

It was in that year that he moved to SS Cars as chief development engineer though, early in 1941, he transferred to Bristol Aero Engines and carburetter development but he was back with SS at Foleshill in 1943. Together with Heynes and Claude Baily, they conceived the XK twin overhead camshaft engine that would power every Jaguar car between 1951 and 1971. In 1950 Hassan departed for Coventry Climax where he was subsequently responsible for no less than thirty different types of engines of which the most celebrated was the World Championship winning V8 of 1958–1964. Hassan returned to Jaguar in 1966 as Group Chief Engineer, Power Plant, and stayed on beyond his retirement age to see the V12 into production and retired, aged sixty-seven in April 1972.

ports located between the camshafts, with carburetters, or injectors, placed directly above the head. The four cam V12 also had hemispherical combustion chambers, similar to those used in the XK engine. But while he had been at Coventry Climax, Hassan had gained considerable experience of using a cylinder-head with a completely flat surface and Jaguar began experiments with single cylinder engines with comparative heads. 'A spy in our workshops in the mid-1960s might have thought we intended to break into the high performance motor cycle market, for he would have noticed several water cooled singles throbbing away, and very few V12s.'

This work culminated in the conclusion that the flat-headed engine was more suitable for the touring car than the hemispherical one. This was initially found to be puzzling but the reason was, Hassan felt, '... that whereas the XK was a long stroke design in all its most famous forms, the oversquare 2.4 and the near square 2.8-litre were never as satisfactory. My interpretation is that a hemispherical head is better when allied to a long stroke unit, and not so good for a short stroke layout, unless sheer maximum power is required.'

With flat cylinder-heads, and single as opposed to four camshafts, the V12 could be relied upon to provide smooth, consistent power up to 6,500rpm, although this was a little high for the Borg-Warner automatic transmission on the touring version. By contrast, the four cam unit, capable of reaching 7,000 to 8,000rpm, would have been unusable in this context on a road car.

On the other hand William Heynes and Claude Baily were keen advocates of the twin cam layout which was, of course, instantly identifiable with the Jaguar marque. But an internal costing on the respective capital investment for the two engines, inevitably showed that the simpler single cam V12 unit was cheaper, requiring £420,000, compared with £491,000 for the twin. When parts and labour were taken into considera-

tion, this worked out at £24 per engine for the single cam, as opposed to close on £42 for the more complex twin. In addition, the single cam layout was a better proposition as far as the increasingly important consideration of emissions requirements were concerned.

'Sir William took a neutral and, in my view, absolutely correct view about this: at the end of the day he wanted an engine of which he could be proud ... one which would perform well, be ultra-refined and one which by its appearance would maintain an aura of the Jaguar image he had spent so many years building up', says Hassan. Lyons drove both cars fitted, respectively, with the four cam head and the flat head single one. At a technical board meeting in 1968, the vote was taken which went in favour of the single cam head. 'By this time it became clear that we could not afford to produce two types of engine ... and this led to the demise of the twin cam cylinder head.'

So the single cam/flat head V12 was chosen for the XJ6 saloon though in 1968, William Heynes recommended that it should first be used to power the E-type, and this is what happened. There was an excellent precedent for this course of action, in that the XK engine was first used in the XK120 sports car of 1948, prior to its fitment in the big Mark VII saloon of two years later. The introduction of the V12 engine would also give the E-type a necessary boost because it would be ten years old in 1971. Although the idea was originally to offer the V12 as an option to the six-cylinder engine the reality was that emissions equipment had so stifled its output that its original 265bhp had fallen back to a mere 171bhp with the attendant dropping off of performance. By 1970 the top speed of the 4.2-litre E-type had slumped to around the 130mph (274khp) mark. Eventually just three six-cylinder Series III E-type would be built though otherwise the model would be exclusively V12-powered. It was hoped to launch the model in the Geneva

*The mid-engined, V12-powered XJ13 was completed by
Jaguar in 1966 as a Le Mans contender but was never to run
there due to a crash in 1971. It was superbly rebuilt and
completed in 1973. It is shown here in its rejuvenated form, the
flares on the wheelarches being the give-away!*

Motor Show which opened on 11 March 1971,
which is where the XJ13 came in.

THE RETURN OF THE XJ13

The idea was to take a party of motoring
journalists for a meal at a suitably rural
hostelry and the proceedings would be interrupted by the far away roar of a V12 engine,
which would get progressively closer and the
hitherto unseen XJ13 would then burst
forth from the surrounding forest, so dramatically announcing the new V12 power unit.

An intrinsic part of the plan was a pro-
motional film of the car and, on Wednesday
20 January 1971, the XJ13 was taken to the

MIRA circuit where with Jaguar's test driver
Norman Dewis at the wheel, it was filmed at
speed. When this had been completed, Dewis
was making a final lap when something
happened to a rear wheel or tyre. The car
went over the banking and was sprung
against the retaining fence, whereupon it
rolled back down the track and came to rest
in the ploughed field in the centre of the
circuit. Fortunately Dewis suffered little
less than a stiff neck but it looked as though
the car was a write-off. It was returned to
Browns Lane and there it remained for a
further two years.

Sir William Lyons had retired in his
seventieth year in 1972 and his place was
taken by 'Lofty' England. He decided to
initiate a rebuild of the XJ13 as, on investi-

A close-up of the V12's combined rear-light and flasher unit.

gation, it was found that its all important centre section had not been badly damaged in the accident. And as luck would have it, Jaguar still had the body formers, which by chance had been stored outside a storeroom for obsolete components at Jaguar's Radford factory. Had they remained inside they would have been scrapped, making the rejuvenation prohibitively expensive. They were returned to Abbey Panels, which had made the original body, and the work was completed in time for the British Grand Prix at Silverstone in July 1973. There England drove the car – which was the first that the British public knew of its existence. However, Australian enthusiasts had known of the XJ13 a good eighteen months previously because *Wheels* magazine had published details and a photograph of the car in February 1972 though it was incorrectly described

This side view of the V12 roadster clearly shows that the space between the back of the seats and the bodywork was amply filled by the lowered hood.

The Series III was the only E-type to be fitted with a grille over the air intake, while there was additional ducting below.

A close-up of the V12's Dunlop pressed steel wheels. Originally, the Series III was fitted with SP Sport radial ply tubeless tyres from the same manufacturer.

Harry Mundy (1914–1988)

The development, with Wally Hassan, of the V12 Jaguar engine represented the culmination of Harry Mundy's impressive and varied engineering career, which embraced road and racing engines and technical journalism.

Born in the city of Coventry, he was educated at King Henry VIII public school and, in 1930, joined the Alvis company in Holyhead Road, where he served his engineering apprenticeship though he left in 1936 for ERA. Mundy worked for the firm until it ran into financial difficulties in 1939 and moved on to be senior designer at Morris Engines at Coventry.

During the 1939–1945 war, Mundy was an engineering officer and an acting Wing Commander in the Royal Air Force and, after hostilities, joined BRM, the spiritual successor of ERA, as head of the design office. There he was in the eye of the storm surrounding Peter Berthon's controversial V16 Formula 1 engine. Dissatisfied by the problems at Bourne, Mundy contemplated joining Jaguar but, in 1950, was recruited by his friend Hassan (they had both known the Gray brothers who built ERA bodies) to become chief designer of Coventry Climax Engines. Working in tandem, the pair produced the highly successful FWA competition engine of 1954, which was to dominate small sports car racing in its day.

Mundy stayed at Widdrington Road until 1955, when he left to join *The Autocar* and became the magazine's first technical editor. It was while at Dorset House that Harry found time to create what was to become the Lotus Twin Cam engine (originally conceived for the Facel Vega Facellia) though, in view of its success, cursed himself for having undertaken the commission for a fee rather than a royalty.

After nine years with *Autocar*, in 1964 the peppery Mundy was eventually lured back to the motor industry to become Jaguar's Executive Director (Power Unit Design). Once again working in harness with his old friend and colleague Hassan, Jaguar's V12 entered production in 1971. Mundy remained at Jaguar until his retirement in 1980.

SIGNIFICANT V12-ENGINED ROAD CARS, 1915–1971

1915 Packard Twin Six, 6.9-litre, sv (USA)
1927 Daimler Double Six, 7.1-litre, slv (UK)
1929 Maybach Zeppelin, 7.9-litre, ohv (G)
1930 Cadillac Twelve, 6-litre, ohv (USA)
1931 Hispano-Suiza Type 68, 9.4-litre, ohv (F)
1932 Lincoln KB, 7.2-litre, hz (USA)
1932 Auburn Twelve, 6.2-litre, hz (USA)
1935 Lincoln Zephyr, 4.3-litre, sv (USA)
1935 Rolls-Royce Phantom 111, 7.3-litre, ohv (UK)
1937 Lagonda V12, 4.5-litre, sohc (UK)
1947 Ferrari 125 Sport, 1.5-litre, sohc (I)
1964 Lamborghini 350 GT, 3.5-litre, tohc (I)
1971 Jaguar E-type, 5.3-litre, sohc (UK)

Key:

hz – horizontal valves
sohc – single overhead camshaft
ohv – overhead valve
sv – side valve
slv – sleeve valve
tohc – twin overhead camshafts
F – France
G – Germany
I – Italy
UK – United Kingdom
USA – United States of America

Totals by country:

USA – 5
United Kingdom – 4
Italy – 2
France – 1
Germany – 1

as the 'Secret F-type'! But, in many respects, the XJ13 marked the ending of a chapter in the Jaguar story. It was the last competition car to be built by the factory. Thereafter such work would be assigned to an outside contractor.

THE V12 E-TYPE

In view of the XJ13 catastrophe, the launch of the Series III E-type was switched to Palm Beach, underlining the fact that America

Browns Lane, in the dark days of 1976. Pictured from left to right: Ronald Barker of Car *Magazine, plant director Peter Craig, Harry Mundy, the author, Mrs George Lanchester and Rodney Walkerley, former sports editor of* Motor.

was to be the model's principal market. The event, held on 25 March 1971, was attended by Sir William Lyons, on what was to be a farewell journey to the United States. He was accompanied by one of the architects of the V12 engine, Harry Mundy.

As announced in Britain, the Series III V12-powered E-type was made in a single length of the 2 + 2's 8ft 9in (2.67m) wheelbase and the open two-seater version was therefore discontinued. In roadster form the V12 cost £3,123 while the coupe sold for £3,369, which in both instances was £256

more than the equivalent Series III six-cylinder cars which were listed though, as already noted, not subsequently offered for public sale. The use of the 5.3-litre V12 pushed the car's top speed up to 145mph (233kph) though the impedimenta of American de-toxing equipment meant that trans-Atlantic versions were only capable of about 135mph (217khp). In the case of the non-US cars, acceleration was a noticeable improvement on that of the six, with the latter capable of reaching that figure in 7.2 seconds while the V12 clipped this to 6.4

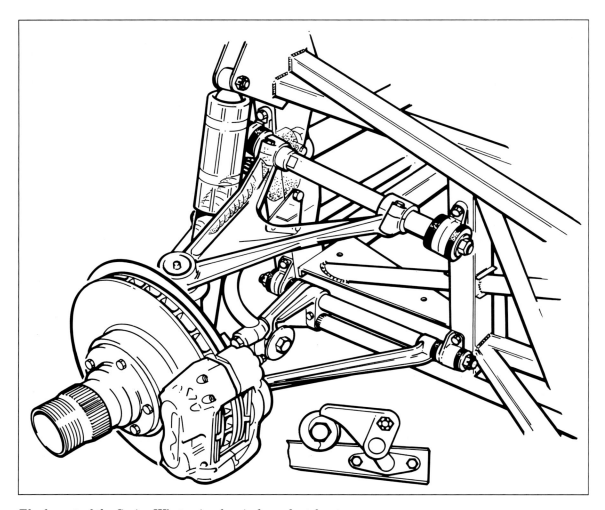

The layout of the Series III's torsion bar independent front-suspension was essentially that of its predecessors though featured anti-dive geometry and ventilated discs. The inset shows the snail-type adjuster to vary the car's ride height.

seconds though, once again, the Federalised version was actually slower at 7.4 seconds.

Externally, the V12 E-type was easily identifiable by its enlarged air intake, which was fitted with a chromed grille for the first time. New pressed steel painted wheels with chromed hub caps were fitted as standard though the more traditional wire wheels were also available at extra cost. They were also larger than hitherto, with 6in (152mm)

rather than 5in (127mm) rims. Both the front and rear arches were flared to accommodate them.

All-important modifications were made to the E-type's structure to accommodate the V12 though the basic monocoque tub/triangulated engine/suspension framework was perpetuated. In view of the fact that the new engine weighed 680lb (308kg), which was 80lb (36kg) more than the six-cylinder

XK unit, gusset plates were introduced to the framework at the junction of the upper tubes while a tubular tiebar was introduced beneath the engine. It was possible to reduce the turning circle of the steering from 42 to 36ft (13 to 11m).

The front track was also modestly increased, from 50 to 54.6in (1,270 to 1,387mm). Front-suspension was essentially unchanged, apart from the pivot line of the upper wishbone, which was realigned to create an anti-dive effect, and followed in the wheel tracks of the newly introduced XJ6 saloon. The upper wishbones received Slip-flex sealed for life bearings while snail cams replaced the vernier adjusters on the front torsion bars. At the rear of the car, the independent suspension remained essentially the same though the track was increased from 50 to 53in (1,270 to 1,346mm) with wishbones from the discontinued 420G fitted. More powerful brakes than hitherto were employed and were 11.18in (18mm) diameter ventilated discs and were a substantial 0.94in (2mm) thick. At the rear the inboard discs were enlarged to 10.38in (17mm) diameter. Jaguar also took the opportunity to introduce under body ductings to cool the differential; always an E-type bugbear. An enlarged petrol tank was fitted, which increased capacity from 14 (64) to 18 gallons (82 litres).

But the heart of the Series III E-type was of course, the 5.3-litre engine which was the only V12 of its day to be produced in volume and, in the first year, Jaguar planned to build 9,100 units. It was the first mass-produced V12 since the Lincoln Zephyr engine of the 1936–1948 era. Although in Italy both Ferrari and Lamborghini manufactured V12s these were relatively low production units. Jaguar spent £3 million on tooling-up its Radford factory to produce the new engine. No less than £850,000 were expended on three Archdale transfer machines for machining the alloy cylinder block while £700,000 went on a 42 station Huller trans-

fer machines for equivalent head operations. Engine assembly was carried out on a 52 stage track and, after testing, they were then transferred to Browns Lane by lorry for installation into the E-type's body. Unlike the six, which was introduced to the car from underneath, the V12 was fitted into the car from above.

The four cam 4,994cc racing engine had been limited to a capacity of 5 litres to permit it to run at Le Mans, but there were no such constraints for the road-going version and the bore size was accordingly upped from 87 to 90mm. The 70mm stroke was retained and this gave a capacity of 5,343cc. The massive crankcase was of LM25 manganese molybdenum with an open deck at the top with the cast-iron liners pushed, in the Italian manner, into deep spigots in the jacket floor. As will be recalled, Jaguar's previous experience with aluminium XK blocks, as used on the lightweight cars, had not been particularly happy and the V12's crankcase was extended 4in (102mm) below the centre line of the bearings to add to the rigidity on the case.

The substantial three plane crankshaft of EN 16T steel was unusual for a modern V12 in that it was a forging whereas in view of the relatively small numbers involved, its Ferrari and Laborghini contemporaries used

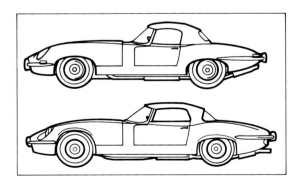

The Series III convertible with raised hood (top) or fitted with hard-top with the benefits of its large rear window readily apparent.

The Series III coupe (1972 model) in Moscow's Red Square.
The V12 E-type perpetuated the wheelbase of the earlier 2 + 2
model.

shafts machined from a solid billet. It ran in seven main bearings and, while the engine was under development, there were fears that the engine would suffer from bearing rumble. So an alternative cast-iron crankcase was produced, which added 116lb (53kg) to the engine's weight and, fortunately, such fears proved unfounded and it was not used. Each cylinder bank actuated its valves by a single overhead camshaft driven by a duplex chain, which was no less than 5.5ft (1.67m) long, running from a sprocket on the nose of the crankshaft. It also powered a jackshaft located in the middle of the V which, in turn, drove the distributor.

Since the early 1960s, racing engines had employed neoprene cogged belts to drive camshafts and ancillaries which were cheaper and quieter than traditional chains. In 1961, the German Glas company had introduced such a belt for the first time on an overhead camshaft engine of a road car. Fiat had followed in 1967 with its 124 Sport model, where such a belt was employed to drive the twin overhead camshafts on its four-cylinder engine. Jaguar, maybe sensing that it might be accused of being ultra conversative by adopting chains on the V12, in the press pack it released with the engine's announcement, posed the question: 'Isn't chain drive a little outdated?' I can do no better than quote the reply, which mentioned that Jaguar had considerable experience of chain drive and pointed out that: 'You can only use one side of a belt to drive most of your components whereas with a chain you can use both. Therefore, with a belt drive, you would need at least two belts to drive even the minimum number of components and, since quite a wide belt is needed to withstand the loads reliably, this form of drive would have increased the overall length of the engine by quite an amount. It's long enough as it is!'

As far as the cylinder heads were concerned, these were aluminium with in-line valves though the inlet was larger at 1.625in (41mm) head diameter than the 1.375in (35mm) exhaust. Twin valves springs were fitted and the tappets and camshaft operated, in the Coventry Climax manner, in a separate tappet block. This permitted the shaft and tappet to be made from a material with good bearing properties and such a construction simplified the casting and machining of the heads themselves. Tappet clearances were by the usual Jaguar system of inserting shims between the valve stem and an inverted cup. The faces of the cylinder heads were completely flat, which greatly simplified and cheapened the production and machining processes. As a result the pistons contained the combustion chamber, which consisted of a shallow depression in the crown with a clearly defined periphery.

No less than four Zenith Stromberg 175 CD carburetters were fitted. It will be recalled that the racing four cam V12 had its carburetters mounted directly above the block. The single cam/flat head V12 was experimentally fitted with short inlet manifolds which conveniently fitted into the V but the engine would not produce enough low and medium torque with such an arrangement. Though the problem was resolved by the fitment of 11in (279mm) long inlet tracts which provided a ram effect, less desirably, the side-mounted carburetters increased the width of the engine.

Initially a petrol injection system had been envisaged for the V12 and although a mechanical Lucas system, as used on some lightweight E-types, was tried this proved unable to meet all important emissions requirements. It was replaced by Brico Engineering's electronic system, which seemed ideal and met the legislation. Unfortunately for Jaguar the Coventry company then decided not to put the system into production and conventional carburetters were fitted in its stead. This was particularly regrettable because the more efficient Brico system produced 30 to 40 more bhp than the carburetters that were eventually used. The V12 would be fuel injected, though not until 1975, when it was powering the XJ12 saloon but by that time the E-type had ceased production. A 9:1 compression ratio was employed, reduced from 10.6:1, for a cleaner exhaust.

When the four camshaft V12 engine was undergoing evaluation, problems were experienced with using two six-cylinder distributors and the V12 Jaguar engine was the first power unit to be fitted with Lucas' new Oscillating Pick up System (OPUS) which had been initially developed for Formula 1 racing cars. This was a transistorised design which relied on magnetic impulses and, above all, dispensed with the hitherto conventional mechanical make and break arrangement. This once again helped the engine to meet American pollution legislation.

Those engines destined for the US market were fitted with an air injection system supplied by a pump, belt-driven off the nose of the crankshaft. The injector nozzles were located on the manifold side of the exhaust valves. To counter the problem of the rich mixture which could occur when the throttle was closed suddenly, an anti-backfire, or what the Americans called a gulp valve was

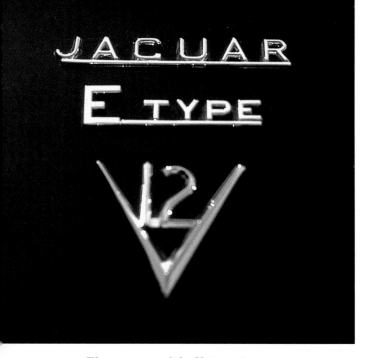

The presence of the V12 engine was underlined by this pronouncement on the boot lid.

employed, so called because it supplied a gulp of air to the inlet manifold which enabled the mixture in the combustion chambers to burn more completely.

Jaguar quoted a figure of 272bhp at 5,800rpm as the output for the 5.3-litre V12, which compared with 265bhp at 5,400rpm for the 4.2-litre XK engine. However, the V12's figure related to the more stringent Deutsche Industry Norm (DIN) formula. If the earlier, and more lenient, SAE rating had been applied, the V12's output would have been quoted at 317bhp at 6,200rpm.

Because of the 2 + 2's longer wheelbase, it became possible to offer automatic transmission for the first time on an E-type roadster. This was a 12J Borg-Warner unit and essentially an uprated version of the gearbox offered on the XJ6 saloon. It was used in conjunction with higher ratios than the 3.31:1 norm, 3.07:1 on cars for the British market and 3.31 on the American one. The manual gearbox was the standard all-synchromesh unit used on the 4.2-litre six since 1964 and conceived at the time with the V12 in mind. However, the V12 has a 10.5in (266mm) diameter clutch rather than a 9.5in (241mm) unit.

In view of the fact that the V12 engine was somewhat heavier than the six-cylinder XK unit, power steering was employed as standard on the Series III, the Adwest system being fitted with the latest collapsible energy-absorbing steering column as demanded by American safety legislation. The use of power steering allowed a smaller steering-wheel than was hitherto possible, thereby increasing the driver's leg room. So out went the traditional wood-rimmed wheel to be replaced by a leather-covered one with the usual satin-finished alloy spokes.

Inside, the coupe version was little changed from its Series II predecessor, though there were some detail changes mostly associated with improving the accommodation. The floor was redesigned and accordingly lowered, taking it to the level of the Series II footwells. On the coupe, changes to the seat mechanism resulted in more foot room for the rear passengers though this still meant children. The longer wheelbase of the roadster meant additional space behind the front seats, which permitted the introduction of a luggage platform behind the seats incorporating a luggage bin.

The concept of exposed headlamps, introduced on the Series I½ E-type, was continued on its V12-powered successor. Quartz halogen lamps were also available at extra cost.

V12 E-TYPE AND ITS CONTEMPORARIES, APRIL 1971

Make/model	Top speed	Price
AC 428	140mph (225kph)	£ 7,575
Aston Martin DBS V8	145mph (233kph)	£ 5,501
Bristol 411	135mph (217kph)	£ 7,872
Chevrolet Corvette	120mph (193kph)	£ 5,094
Ferrari 365GT 2 + 2	150mph (241kph)	£ 9,141
Jaguar Series III E-type open two-seater	146mph (234kph)	£ 3,123
Jaguar Series III E-type fixed-head coupe	142mph (228kph)	£ 3,369
Lamborghini Miura	170mph (273kph)	£10,860
Maserati Indy	155mph (249kph)	£ 8,190
Porsche 911	125mph (201kph)	£ 3,671

THE SERIES III E-TYPE IN THE PRESS

But how was the Series III E-type received by the motoring press of the day and how did it compare with its six-cylinder predecessor? In its issue of 27 November 1971 *Motor* published its findings on a V12-powered roadster, registration number VKV 881J, fitted with a factory hard-top.

ROAD TEST
Jaguar E-type V12
Reproduced from *Motor* 27 November 1971

Our test car ... managed 146 mph a shade slower all out than the original 3.8 XK. In terms of power/weight, though, the V12 is the quickest E-type yet, reaching 100 mph in just 15.4 sec compared with 17.2 of the 4.2 coupe...

Nor is the E-type now the sports car it used to be – other purpose-built machines can corner faster and handle more entertainingly though they are mostly more expensive. But if not beyond criticism it is still in a class of its own for sheer performance and value for money.

Performance and economy
The starter needs to turn the V12 over several times before sufficient petrol/air has found its way down the long induction pipes to fire; the choke can almost immediately be pushed from the full to the halfway position and it doesn't need much time for the running temperature to be reached. The warm-up period is untemperamental and stammer-free.

With most V12s one is very conscious of the term 'on song' – both aurally and with reference to the camshaft. The Jaguar V12 unit needs no such euphemism. It develops over 250lb.ft. of torque from 1300–5700 rpm peaking at 304lb.ft. at 3600 rpm, so its top gear performance is really remarkable; it gives a steady surge of power all the way with no suggestion of getting on the cam – it never gets off it and will pull evenly from under 500 rpm with an almost automatic transmission quality. In fact a close inspection of the figures shows the best top gear pull from 40–80 mph where each 10 mph step takes 2.8 seconds; in third gear the best period is from 40.70 mph each 10 mph taking just 1.8 seconds. So there is some evidence of getting on the step but subjectively the pull feels even from 20 to 120 mph.

With such torque there is little need to wind the engine up in the gears but if you need to hang onto a gear during overtaking, the red line occurs at 6500 rpm – valve crash is apparent at 7850 rpm. From tickover to around 5000 rpm the engine is virtually inaudible – wind-rush around the hardtop

*This 1971 Series III V12-powered E-type is instantly
identifiable by the combination of flared wheelarches and disc
– as opposed to wire – wheels, though the latter were available
at extra cost. This is the convertible fitted with the optional
black glass fibre hard-top, and its own ventilation outlet.*

drowns most of the top-end noise – but
beyond 5000 rpm you can begin to hear a
smooth purr, changing to a harsher more
mechanical sound over 6000. It is very well
insulated from the cockpit and the engine
seems completely vibration free. Most of us
would have liked a more obvious V12 sound
from the four tail pipes.

Although the outright maximum speed is
down on that of the old 4.2, the standing start
accelerations are much better. The maximum
varies as the cube root of power, while
acceleration, until drag takes charge, is a
straight function of power to weight, and in
that the V12 is significantly superior. Leaving black trails on the start line, the V12
reaches 50 mph in 4.7 seconds, 100 mph in
15.4 and 120 mph in 25.8 compared with 4.8,

17.2 and 25.2sec for the old 4.2 showing
where the extra drag begins to affect the V12.
At 14.5 mpg the fuel consumption is heavy; it
seemed to make little difference whether the
car was driven at home or abroad.

Local driving and hard acceleration returned much the same 15 mpg as continuous
100 mph cruising on French autoroutes; it
wasn't till the maximum speed testing and
faster return journey with 115 mph cruising
that the consumption dropped to 13 mpg.
With this sort of running the maximum
range of the 18 gallon [81 litres] tank is only
just over 200 miles or two hours' worth.
Although it suffered a little running-on with
French Super fuel, the equivalent 4-star fuel
in Britain produced no trouble.

Transmission

With such massive torque on tap the gearbox is almost unnecessary for normal driving. Even in top gear the overtaking potential is enormous. Even so, a lower gear means less time on the wrong side of the road, so one can still finish up using the gearbox just like a Mini-dicer. It responds pretty well to such treatment. It is a quite firm change with powerful synchromesh and you have to concentrate to make gear swaps smooth. There is a lot of friction in a big V12 and as the 'flywheel effect' is pretty small, the revs drop quite quickly in neutral; guaranteed smoothness was achieved with a rapid double declutch on up changes but the change wasn't that much slower if one deliberately feathered the throttle during a single clutch movement. At 45lb. the clutch is heavy but the angle of attack is not good so the effort required is not uncomfortably high.

The gear ratios themselves would do credit to any hot Mini; first is low enough for a contemptuous take-off on a 1 in 3 hill but still good for 55 mph. Second at 6500 rpm takes you to 84 mph and third was something of a luxury in this country, second to top or even first to top were frequent ratio paths without detracting from satisfaction or smoothness. Abroad third gear was a splendid overtaking ratio used frequently on motorways just for the pleasure of the instant surge of power.

Our test car was fitted with the optional 3.07 final drive ratio (the standard one is 3.3), sacrificing a little all-out acceleration for even more long-legged cruising on Continental motorways. A five-speed box would be nice though hardly necessary. Like the gearbox, the limited slip differential incorporated in the final drive was quiet.

Handling and brakes

The E-type used to be a classic sports car, but as the mid-engined sports racer has developed and certain specialist production cars have followed suit, the appeal of the E has changed; its character has softened.

Wheels and tyres sizes have increased considerably too, so the steering effort is much greater than on the old 185–15 tyres; which explains why power steering is not only necessary but part of the car's new character.

E-steering is heavier than XJ6-steering but in our view it is still much too light for a set-up which is so responsive. Making it heavier would not only allow some feel to sense changing adhesion at the front end but also make the car easier to place accurately when correcting any tail slide.

With its improved roadholding the E can still out corner an earlier model but it is difficult to get the ultimate from the chassis. Its characteristics are mostly rail-like cornering with understeer which can be overcome on tighter corners with power, although the limited slip differential keeps the back well under control. At high speeds it runs true but twitches a little at the front in strong side winds – not sufficiently to slow you down particularly, just keeps you alert. Bumps didn't upset its directional stability.

With the Series 3 came anti-dive braking and ventilated front discs. Powerful assistance means that only 60lb. is needed for a 1g stop and we were quite happy with their general feel – we don't cane brakes in normal motoring although engine braking with a high geared slippery-bodied E-type is not very strong. Our fade tests with $20\frac{1}{2}$g stops from 93 mph at one-minute intervals produced some smell and occasional smoke as the car came to rest but didn't require increased pedal pressure. We got the impression that a rapid Alpine descent might fade them but for normal quick motoring they are quite adequate. The handbrake needed adjustment to hold the car both up and down on a 1 in 3 but it still gave 0.34g from 30 mph.

Comfort and controls

Over the years it has frequently been cars with sporting pretensions that have set new ride standards thanks largely to a full understanding of independent suspension systems.

This 1974 V12 is fitted with a manual gearbox, as opposed to the automatic transmission which was a popular option on the Series III.

Head-restraints were often fitted as standard on export V12s, though they were an optional extra on British-sold examples.

The E-type has always taken wavy surfaces very smoothly – and still does. With little potential weight variation, spring and damper settings don't have to be the compromise that they are in saloons so the E-type can be set fairly taut without getting wallowy when laden with passenger and luggage. On broken surfaces it is a bit rattly although much of this on our car came from the hood folded up behind the front seats. When it is pressed to its limit on corners some roll is evident from the outside but it isn't noticeable inside.

To use high cornering power you need very good seat location, otherwise you finish up by hanging onto the steering wheel. This is particularly true of a car with power steering which offers little bracing resistance. The comfortable seats provide some sideways location but they could do with still more which could be provided without upsetting access. Leather upholstery doesn't assist grip very much either. Unfortunately there isn't room for a clutch footrest so you tend to dip your foot underneath the pedal. A hypercritical observation, perhaps, but we feel a decent rest would make fast driving that much easier.

The longer wheelbase has allowed a much greater range of useful seat adjustment; our tame 6ft. 5in. road-tester found there was plenty of room for him to sit comfortably with enough headroom even though the seat is set quite high to allow lesser mortals to see over the bonnet. The steering column is adjustable through a useful range, although it still leaves the indicator/flasher stalk behind and sometimes out of fingertip reach. Apart from the proximity of the clutch pedal to the tunnel the other two pedals are well spaced for conventional heel-and-toe use.

The convertible is understandably noisier at speed than the quiet coupe. At 80 mph there is a little wind noise round the hardtop, more with the soft-top, but as speed increases to the comfortable autoroute cruising gait of 110–115 mph, wind rush begins to drown the radio. By sports car standards it is average.

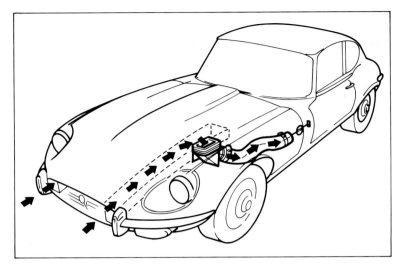
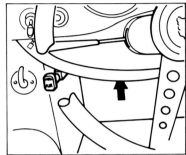

*In 1972 the E-type acquired a much needed fresh air
ventilation system. Ducting was introduced on both sides of the
car, the facility being regulated by pull/push controls.*

At most speeds the engine in top gear is quite
inaudible and it isn't until you get over the
100 mph mark that you begin to notice it,
which all adds to the deceptive quality of E-
type progress. One never hears the exhaust
note unfortunately, unless you have the hood
down and are driving between walls.

Jaguar heating/ventilation was never good
until the XJ6 came along; only some of this
knowledge has been passed on to the Series 3
E-type. There's still no face-level ventilation
but the two in/out controls for temperature
and air volume and the two separate direction controls for passenger and driver can
provide a pleasant atmosphere whatever the
ambient conditions without too much fiddly
adjustment though the levers themselves are
extremely small and difficult to manipulate.
The hardtop incorporates its own outlet vents
which boosts the throughput against previous E-type.

A full wraparound screen at the rear of the
hardtop gives very good over-the-shoulder
visibility and slim front pillars add to the
general feeling of airiness. With the soft top
the clear panel isn't quite as large but the
hood doesn't get in the way at angled junc-
tions.

Fittings and furniture

With its origins in pre-war Jaguars, the facia
is still as open to criticism as before. The
smaller dials are scattered away to the left
and only get the occasional glance while the
fuel gauge is hidden by the left hand. A
battery of four switches on each side of the
side/head pair in the centre look impressive
but are hard to find without looking. You
need to remember the order of switches from
the centre to grope accurately. A right-hand
facia dipswitch is another inconvenience.
Driving along a wet twisty road on a misty
night smoking a cigarette, the ash gets every-
where but in the awkwardly placed ashtray
at the rear of the central console. You need
the right hand for dipping the impressive
lights to their indifferent dip and for holding
the cigarette every now and then while the left
hand changes gear, stabs for the wiper switch
for an occasional flick while the adjacent
finger prods the washer switch. British
Leyland's own Marina is far better in this
respect.

The optional hardtop is held on by three
overcentre clips across the screen top and a
bolt behind each seat, so it is a two-man job
to remove it. The soft top is permanently in

JAGUAR E-TYPE SERIES III SPECIFICATION

PRODUCTION *1971–1973 (Fixed-Head Coupe), 1971–1975 (Roadster)*

ENGINE

Block material	Aluminium alloy
Head material	Aluminium alloy
Cylinders	60 degree V12
Cooling	Water
Bore and stroke	90×70mm
Capacity	5,343cc
Main bearings	7
Valves	2 per cylinder; sohc per cylinder bank
Compression ratio	9:1
Carburetters	4 Zenith 175 CD SE
Max power (net)	272bhp @ 5,850rpm
Max torque	304lb ft 3,600rpm

TRANSMISSION

Clutch:	Single dry plate, hydraulically operated.
Type:	Four speed synchromesh (optional Borg-Warner 12J three speed automatic).

OVERALL GEAR RATIOS   AUTOMATIC

Top	3.07	3.1
3rd	4.27	
2nd	5.86	4.80
1st	9.00	7.93
Reverse	10.37	
Final drive	Salisbury hypoid, Powr-Lok limited slip differential 3.31:1 (automatic 3.07:1).	

SUSPENSION AND STEERING

Front:	Independent, double wishbones incorporating anti-dive geometry longitudinal torsion bars, telescopic dampers, anti-roll bar.
Rear:	Independent, with lower tubular links and fixed length drive shafts for transverse location, longitudinal location by radius arms. Two coil springs and telescopic dampers each side, anti-roll bar.
Steering:	Adwest power assisted rack and pinion.
Tyres:	Dunlop SP Sport.
Wheels:	Dunlop pressed steel.
Rim Size:	6in.

BRAKES

Type:	Girling discs front and rear with Lockheed vacuum servo assistance.
Size:	Front ventilated 11.18in; Rear 10.38in.

DIMENSIONS (in/mm)

Track	
Front:	54.3/1,379
Rear:	53.3/1,353
Wheelbase:	105/2,667
Overall length:	184.4/4,785
Overall width:	66.1/1,678
Overall height:	51.4/1,305
Ground clearance:	5.4/137
Unladen weight:	28.8cwt/1,454kg
Front/Rear weight distribution:	52/48

place and folds down, enclosed in a neat
hoodbag into the well behind. You can still
get some luggage underneath this, but if you
ever need to transport, say, a carry-cot you
need the soft top up when there is quite a
useful platform behind; we even carried a
third adult on that shelf with the passenger's
seat forward. The boot itself is fairly shallow,
as the spare wheel is in a well underneath,
together with tool kit and wheelchanging
equipment. We managed to get 3.8 cu.ft. of
our luggage inside which is just about
enough for an economical grand tour if you
use the space behind the seats. A glove locker
and a parcel shelf (useful on the passenger
side only) supplement the spaces.

*The facia is padded top and bottom and the
cover is attractive non reflecting PVC; a rubber strip is stitched to the carpet for passenger and driver heels...*

Motor's criticism of the V12 heating and
ventilation system were to some extent
answered at the 1972 Geneva Motor Show,
when a supplementary fresh air ventilation
system was introduced to the Series III. Air
was fed from two small intakes introduced
either side of the radiator grille. It passed up
rectangular tubing in the engine compartment and then transferred to a flexible duct
alongside each footwell and entered the car
via a mushroom nozzle. A pull/push knob
under the facia regulated the flow.

Simultaneously Kangol inertia reel seat
belts were standardised on the coupe and
concealed behind the rear trim. This dispensed with the earlier sill mounted units
and made the tailgate release somewhat
easier to operate.

MAXIMUM SPEEDS	mph	kph
Mean of opposite runs	146	235
Best one-way kilometre	149	240
3rd gear	116	187
2nd gear	84	135
1st gear	55	89

ACCELERATION TIMES	
mph	sec
0–30	2.7
0–40	3.5
0–50	4.7
0–60	6.4
0–70	8.0
0–80	9.9
0–90	12.7
0–100	15.4
0–110	19.3
0–120	25.8
Standing quarter mile	14.2
Standing kilometre	26.1

*The only mass-produced V12 engine
of its day being assembled at
Jaguar's Radford factory. The
former Daimler works had been
extensively re-equipped to cater for
the manufacture of the new engine.*

The V12's cockpit. Note the final departure of the wood-rimmed steering-wheel. The all-important plaque signed by Sir William Lyons – indicating the car's special status as one of the last fifty roadsters – can be seen on the lid of the glove compartment.

SUMMARY

So how did the V12 E-type sell during its three and a half year production life? In 1972, the first full year of output, just 3,705 cars, 1,711 roadsters and 1,994 coupes were built. This compared with 9,948 six-cylinder cars made in 1969. Inevitably the vast majority of cars were sent to America, with 2,321 Series III E-types exported in 1972, which

adversely contrasted with no less than 7,456 six-cylinder cars sent across the Atlantic in the heady days of 1969.

Although 4,686 Series IIIs left Browns Lane in 1973, the sands were running out for the V12. There were more stringent American safety regulations pending for 1976, for its boot mounted petrol tank would not have have met a 30mph (48kph) rear-ward barrier crash test. Also, by 1973, the

When the E-type was due to be discontinued, the model was removed from the main production line to a small track at Browns Lane. This is the last car, a Series III roadster, body number 4S 8989. Note that at this stage it was fitted with spoked wheels at the front.

reality was that transatlantic demand for the model had virtually ceased. An undoubted factor was that, although the US designated cars were offered with the option of air conditioning, there was insufficient space under the V12's bonnet to fit a really efficient system. The 2 + 2 ceased production in October 1973, the knock-out blow having been dealt by yet more American legislation, which required that from 1974, coupes be fitted with an internal roll-over bar. But the roadster, which continued, also suffered because the 1974 American designated cars had to be fitted with ungainly rubber bumper overriders to meet increasingly safety orientated laws. These extremities, and their associated metalwork, also added undesirably to the car's weight and immediately detracted from the E-type's ageing but still impressive lines.

If this was not enough, the Arab/Israeli war had broken out in October 1973 and with it came a downturn in the world economy and a spiralling of oil prices. In 1974 E-type output slumped to a mere 2,759 cars and one of 'Lofty' England's last decisions, before his retirement as Jaguar's chairman in January 1974, was to cancel the by then outdated and unfashionably thirsty model. The roadster therefore ceased production in the week ending 14 September 1974, making a total of 14,983 V12s built, almost

The E-type bows out. The last car receives its engine, number 7S 17201 SA. There are rear disc wheels and these were subsequently fitted all round, as the photograph of the completed car, on page 26, shows.

evenly split between 7,975 roadsters and 7,008 coupes. This brought the total of all E-types manufactured to 72,233, produced over a thirteen year production span.

In view of the fact that there was still a considerable number of E-types in dealers' showrooms, news of the model's impending demise was not made public until February 1975. The last fifty right-hand drive cars, from chassis number IS 2823, appropriately black finished, (though the last but one had dark green bodywork to the special order of American Jaguar enthusiast Robert Danny) and sported chromium plated spoked wheels. They were offered at £3,812, which was only £69 more than the production roadster. Each had a dashboard plaque, bearing its number and a facsimile signature of the by then retired Sir William

Lyons. Although many went abroad, the reality was that in Britain the shadow of the depression meant that those cars retained for home sale were to linger in the showrooms for many months and were even on offer for the knock down price of £3,500, showing that the firm's decision to cancel the thirteen-year-old car had been a correct one. However, Jaguar retained the very last car, chassis number IS 2872, for its own collection of historic vehicles.

Seven months later, in September 1975, the Coventry company unveiled its new V12-powered XJ-S Grand Touring coupe, which at £8,900 was the most expensive Jaguar ever and over twice the price of the E-type. But was it the right car and should the firm have replaced the E with the much anticipated F-type sports car?

6 Whatever Happened to the F-type?

'It is clear that the E-type replacement, scheduled for later this year, will be a closed coupe rather than a rugged wind-in-the-hair two-seater.'

Autocar, 8 March 1975

One of the reasons that the last fifty E-types took so long to sell was that the public were expecting the model to be replaced by another sports car. It was what the motoring press continually and speculatively referred to as the F-type. But, as we have seen, what emerged seven months after the E-type's demise was the upmarket XJ-S Grand Touring coupe, which was a totally different type of car. The purpose of this chapter is to see how the 'F' became the S and much credit should go to Jaguar historian Philip Porter, who has managed to untangle and give a sense of progression to what is a far from straightforward story.

As early as 1966, when the E-type had been in production for five years, Jaguar felt that its long bonnet might be rather intimidating for the European market, so Malcolm Sayer produced designs for a rather curious rendering, with a wheelbase cut from 105 to 94in (2.67 to 2.39m) and a foreshortened bonnet with projecting headlights. Perhaps thankfully the idea was not proceeded with. However, probably in 1967, Sayer once again returned to the concept of the 94in (2.39m) wheelbase and schemed out a design for a 2 + 2, unchanged from the bulkhead back, but also with a similar bonnet to the earlier concept and effectively a scaled-down

version of the original. A 3-litre engine was specified and it was also envisaged that 13in (330mm) rather than the usually 15in (381mm) wheels be fitted. Yet another variation was considered, probably in 1968, essentially similar to the first rendering but with a windscreen with far more rake though this particular scheme had the 96in (2.44m) wheelbase of the production two-seater. Thankfully none of these thoughts progressed beyond the drawing board.

Before looking at what were considered to be true E-type replacements, reference must be made to another project mooted in the 1960s, which was undertaken by the British Motor Corporation.

POTENTIAL THREATS

It will be recalled that, in 1966, Jaguar had merged with BMC and had thus become privy to the Corporation's future planning. At that time BMC recognised that the long running Austin Healey 3000, a design that was rooted in the early 1950s, would soon require replacement. It therefore conceived the Austin project XC512, or ADO30 in corporate coding, a sports car intended to be powered by the 4-litre Rolls-Royce engine then fitted to the slow selling Vanden Plas Princess R saloon of 1964. ADO30's coupe body was an uneasy amalgam of Pininfarina and Longbridge influences, while suspension was all-independent Hydrolastic units of the type developed for the 1,800cc saloon.

In theory, this would have represented a formidable challenge to the E-type in America. But the reality was that the project was a non-starter and, according to Donald Healey's son, Geoffrey, who saw the car, recalls it being derogatorily described as 'The Thing', 'The Monster' or more memorably 'Fireball XL5'. Despite this, work continued on the project though it was soon recognised that the overhead inlet/side exhaust Rolls-Royce engine did not develop sufficient power for a sports car. Rolls-Royce then developed a new overhead valve cylinder head for the unit but the BMC/Jaguar alliance of 1966 resulted in a scheme being conceived for an XK-engined version with a 3-litre power unit and different suspension – in this instance, courtesy of the MGC. There were additional schemes for Daimler 2½ and 4½ versions. Once again these ideas did not progress beyond the paper stage because thankfully, 'Fireball XL5' was cancelled, according to Healey, after '... a well-known motoring journalist tried the car on a track. He soon convinced the perpetrators of the Monster that its road-holding and handling were diabolical.' So XC512 disappeared from the scene, having absorbed approximately £1 million of corporate funding.

Lyons is rumoured to have had a hand in the demise of ADO30 which, in reality, did not begin to represent a threat to the E-type. But later he was responsible for killing a more formidable challenger to the model in the shape of a mid-engined Rover, powered by the firm's soon to be introduced Buick-based 3.5-litre V8 engine. Created by the talented duo of Spen King and Gordon Bashford in 1966, it was designated P6B and could well have been marketed under the Alvis badge, Rover having taken over that

company in 1965. But in 1967, Rover itself was bought by Leyland and the creation of British Leyland in the following year meant that the once rival Rover and Jaguar companies were in common ownership. Lyons immediately saw the P6B as representing a very real threat to the E-type, which he made very clear to corporation's chairman, Lord Stokes. John Barber, at this time British Leyland's finance director, who drove the Rover, recalls the circumstances of the model's demise: 'It was a super car... But it was pressure from Lyons that cooked it. Bill was a very nice man but he only thought Jaguar. He wasn't very interested in British Leyland and he was afraid that Rover would damage Jaguar. He kept on and on about it, so it was dropped.'

LOOKING FOR A SUCCESSOR

All the projects previously referred to were simply developments on the existing E-type hull. Contemporary with these developments were the XJ21 project, on which work began in about 1966. The first scheme, dated October 1966, still clearly resembles the E-type with the same 105in (2,667mm) wheelbase though with a two inch wider track at 52in (1,321mm). Identified as Body Type A, it was a development of the 2 + 2 E-type and featured a modified nose and windscreen with pronounced rake. Body Type B, of January 1967, had an alternative nose and air intake, and wider rear wings. Although this was a coupe, Sayer also set down a convertible version. He penned yet a further open variation in March 1967, when there were thoughts about the open car with both 2 + 2 and standard wheelbase.

By 1967–1968 Jaguar's thoughts about its future models were beginning to gel and were set down in an internal company document. It included no less than four future sports cars. Initially there was a long wheel-

Although it was thought that the E-type would be replaced by an F-type sports car, instead in 1975 came the up-market Malcolm Sayer-styled XJ-S grand tourer. This is a 1979 car.

base roadster, which would be 5.3-litre V12-powered, with an alternative 3.5-litre V8 derivative also available. Next came a two-seater coupe with bodywork bearing the distinctive rear 'flying buttresses' which were later to emerge on the XJ-S. This would be powered by the same pair of engines. A 2 + 2 version was essentially the then current E-type though with the same eight- and twelve-cylinder variants. Then came a totally new model, described as a 'four-seater sports sedan'. Also known as the XJ 3-litre GT, this

was a smaller car with a 96in (2.44m) wheelbase, distinctive twin headlamps and truncated Kamm tail. Projected power units were 2.5-litre Daimler or 3.5-litre Jaguar V8s. In reality, it was only the V12-powered E-type that reached production status. The V8 version of the V12 was also side-lined because this 60 degree engine never ran satisfactorily.

Up until this point, all the XJ21 schemes were essentially variations on the existing E-type shape but, by 1968, Malcolm Sayer

Transport for a speed king. Donald Campbell's appropriately blue 4.2-litre E-type coupe pictured outside his Surrey home early in 1966. Alongside is a mock-up of his latest Bluebird, a Mach 1.1 jet-powered car.

The Bertone-styled 2 + 2-based Pirana attracted plenty of attention on its appearance at the 1967 Motor Show. Its angular profile was to inspire Malcolm Sayer for the lines of the unseen but projected XJ21 E-type replacement.

clearly began to be influenced by the sharper, crisper lines of contemporary Italian sports cars.

Perhaps one of the most influential was that of the one-off Bertone-styled, E-type-based Pirana, displayed at the 1967 Motor Show and commissioned by the *Daily Telegraph* newspaper's *Weekend Telegraph* colour magazine. It was a theme which was perpetuated on the Lamborghini Espada, also the work of Bertone's celebrated chief stylist, Marcello Gandini, which appeared at the 1968 Geneva Motor Show. A batch of Jaguar drawings executed at this time show this influence. It appears that the XJ21's design was finalised in 1968, the intention being to produce it in 2 + 2 and open versions on the same 105in (2.67m) wheelbase of the 2 + 2. Instructions were issued to the Pressed Steel Company to begin work on the body tooling, with a view to the XJ21 entering production in September 1970.

So far so good but, on 14 November 1968, chief engineer William Heynes set down his thoughts to Sir William Lyons in a document headed: 'E-type Vehicle Project Plan'. As already mentioned, Heynes was convinced that the V12 engine should first be used in the E-type, prior to its fitment in the XJ12 saloon.

The intention was to introduce the V12 E-type, designated XJ25, in January 1970 with the XJ21 following in February 1971. But the V12 engine was running behind schedule and, in view of this, it was subsequently decided to go ahead with the V12-powered E-type, which duly appeared in March 1971. However, this meant by-passing the XJ21 altogether and moving straight on to the V12-engined XJ-S. Two months before, on 9 September, Malcolm Sayer had sent Sir William his ideas for a '... 2 + 2 sports car based on XJ4 parts'. This represented the starting point of what Jaguar internally designated as the XJ27 and what was to emerge as the XJ-S in September 1975.

The Pirana

Although there have been attempts by a number of coachbuilders to offer their interpretations on the E-type theme, perhaps the most successful example was displayed at the 1967 London Motor Show when the Bertone-bodied, E-type-based Pirana was unveiled for the first time.

Commissioned by the *Daily Telegraph* newspaper's colour magazine, the Pirana was conceived just eight months prior to its Earls Court debut. The occasion was the Geneva Motor Show in March when a group of motoring journalists began thinking about the ultimate exotic car which incorporated the best of Lamborghini, Aston Martin, Ferrari, Maserati and Jaguar. A key participant was Courtenay Edwards, the magazine's motoring correspondent, and back in London the idea was taken up by the supplement's editor, John Anstey. He decided that the dream could become a reality, with the resulting car proclaiming the Speed with Luxury theme.

Sir William Lyons was approached and he agreed to sell the *Telegraph* a 4.2-litre 2 + 2 underframe while the Turin-based Bertone company was prepared to undertake the design and construction of the body and have the car ready for that year's London Motor Show. The Pirana's body was the work of Bertone's chief stylist, Marcello Gandini, who already had the lines of the fabled Lamborghini Miura to his credit. Further assistance came from such British firms as Triplex, who supplied the Sundym glass; electrical equipment manufacturer Lucas and Smiths Industries, who produced the air conditioning system and assisted with the instruments.

The car was completed on time for the London show, which opened on 18 October, where, displayed on the Bertone stand, it proved to be a major attraction. The hatchback theme of the 2 + 2 was perpetuated though the Pirana had a distinctive Kamm tail and was finished in a shimmering acrylic silver, flecked with particles of aluminium. The following month Bertone displayed the Pirana at the Turin show. Later it crossed the Atlantic for exhibition in New York and Montreal and survives today in a private British collection.

As the Pirana showed, styling had moved on since the E-type's lines were conceived in the late 1950s. By 1969, the model was clearly in need of replacement. This is a Series II American specification car of that year.

THE XJ-S

Thoughts of a 'luxury type sports car' had first appeared in a memorandum William Heynes submitted to Sir William Lyons in 1963, following the creation of an experimental E-type-based four-seater coupe in 1961. This same project also represented the starting point of no less than two further

Left: *It was not until 1988 that the XJ-S became available in convertible form in addition to the coupe. Both are still available at the time of writing (1989) while the long-anticipated F-type sports car waits in the wings.*

models, the 2 + 2 E-type as mentioned in Chapter 3, and what was dubbed project XJ4, which would finally appear as the XJ6 saloon of 1968.

As a project totally unrelated to that of the E-type, the XJ-S was created with two quite distinctive parameters firmly in place, which dictated its size and body type. Firstly, there was the considerable financial inducement to base the car on the floorpan of the new XJ6 saloon and its running gear. Secondly, there was the ever present sceptre of the all-important American safety regulations which, at that time, were thought would render the open car obsolete. As it transpired, these proposals were cancelled in 1974 but not before the XJ-S was too far advanced to be initially offered in open form, as was British Leyland's controversial Triumph TR7 corporate sports car, which also appeared in 1975. Malcolm Sayer was responsible for the XJ27's lines though they differed radically from those of the C, D and E-types. The body was dominated at the rear by twin 'flying buttresses' of the type which had first appeared on the one-off Pininfarina-bodied Ferrari Dino 206S Speciale at the 1965 Paris Motor Show and finally emerged on the production Dino of 1967. It will be recalled that they had initially cropped up on a revised version of a proposed E-type 2 + 2.

Sadly Malcolm Sayer died in July 1970, aged only fifty-four, and work on the XJ-S was continued by Doug Thorpe, later to become Jaguar's director of styling, and his team. As it happened, Thorpe was unhappy about the rear buttress, and some of the model's other features, but the time factor meant that it was impractical to make any major changes to the car's bodywork and only detail modifications were possible. The XJ-S was based on a 102in (2.59m) wheel-base version of the XJ6's 108in (2.74m) floorpan, achieved by moving the rear-suspension forward. Its engine was the latest version of the 5.3-litre V12 engine, as employed in the Series II XJ12 saloon announced in May 1975, and thus fitted with Lucas fuel injection.

But, above all, with the arrival of the XJ-S in 1975, Jaguar abandoned one plank of its marketing philosophy. For with this model the firm departed, to some extent, from the Lyons value-for-money approach which had been a feature of every car that the company had built since its 1931 inception. At £8,900 the XJ-S was a Supercar, and the most expensive Jaguar ever, though still a good £5,500 less than its contemporary V12-engined Ferrari 365 GT4, which cost £14,584. But from its outset the XJ-S was a

But the XJ21, due to appear in 1970, never arrived and instead, in 1971, came the V12-powered Series III E-type.

controversial car. Its lines were perhaps the least satisfactory of any Jaguar. Not only that. The 150mph (241kph) Grand Tourer was a thirsty car giving a fuel consumption of 14mpg in the 1973 post oil crisis gloom. Although air conditioning was a standard fitment, there was disappointment that the car's interior lacked the traditional wood and leather associated with Jaguar saloons. In fact the XJ-S reflected the plainer interior of the firm's sports cars, as introduced on the XK150 back in 1957 but that, of course, was a considerably cheaper car aimed at a very different and less demanding clientele.

As if this wasn't enough, the same downturn in the world economy was responsible for toppling British Leyland into deficit and, in 1975, the company was nationalised. Tragically for Jaguar, the Ryder Report commissioned by the government recommended that the renamed Leyland Cars be run centrally with the individual plants and corporate identities downgraded. Largely through the efforts of plant manager Peter

Craig, who died suddenly in 1977 and Bob Knight, who had taken over from William Heynes as engineering director in 1969, Jaguar weathered the terrible 1975–1977 era though the latter year saw the arrival of Michael Edwardes as Leyland's new chairman.

JAGUAR INTO THE 1990s

After two years as a far from satisfactory part of the regrouped Jaguar–Rover–Triumph division of the renamed BL Cars, it was Edwardes who, in 1980, appointed forty year old John Egan as Jaguar's chairman, its first for five years. It was a recognition that Jaguar Cars was once again to emerge as a separate entity but 1980 was a year in which the firm built a mere 13,360 cars, its lowest figure since 1957, a reminder that in addition to all the firm's other troubles, the effects of the second, and far more serious oil crisis of 1979, were beginning to bite. Demand for the XJ6 saloon slumped, while customers for the XJ-S were virtually non-existent. When Egan took over, he remembers that: 'They had already stopped making it [the XJ-S]. OK, we once opened the lines to make a few for Canada but in the main it was a very hit and miss, stop and start process.' Egan was determined to keep the S in production and embarked on a drive to improve its quality and that of the mainstream XK6 saloon. In 1981 the high efficiency (HE) version of the V12 engine arrived with a new design of cylinder head, developed by Swiss engineer Michael May, and intended to improve the unit's fuel consumption by around twenty per cent. Jaguar also took the opportunity to introduce a greatly improved interior with burr walnut and leather upholstery very much in evidence. In 1983 the XJ-S was the first recipient of Jaguar's new six-cylinder 3.6-litre, twin overhead camshaft, 24 valve AJ6 en-

Jaguar, Coventry's great survivor

When the E-type was announced in 1961, Jaguar was still a relatively small company which, that year, produced just 24,018 cars. It was dwarfed by the output of the city's mainstream car makers, Rootes and Standard-Triumph, though today Jaguar is the only car manufacturer left in a city which was once the motoring capital of the country.

But back in 1928, when Jaguar's SS predecessors arrived in Coventry, it was home to no less than eight important car makers: Daimler, Hillman, Humber, Riley, Rover, Singer, Standard, Triumph and specialist manufacturers, Alvis, Armstrong Siddeley and Lea-Francis.

By the 1948 Motor Show, where the Jaguar XK120 made its sensational debut and the first to be held after the Second World War, the Coventry scene had changed dramatically. Hillman and Humber were part of the Rootes Group, Triumph was bankrupted and had been taken over by Standard during the war, Rover had left the city and moved to its Solihull shadow factory and an insolvent Riley was absorbed by the Nuffield Organisation and production transferred to the MG factory.

When the E-type had ceased production in 1974, there had been many more casualties. The never robust Lea-Francis company had effectively come to the end of the road in 1953, the last Armstrong Siddeley left the Parkside factory in 1960, Alvis followed in 1967, while the ailing Rootes Group had been totally absorbed by the American Chrysler Corporation in the same year. Jaguar itself had taken over Daimler in 1960 but, from 1968, it and Standard-Triumph were part of British Leyland.

Today, with the exception of Jaguar, Coventry's motor manufacturers have all but disappeared. The last British-designed Triumph was built there in 1980 and although Peugeot, which bought Chrysler's British operations in 1978, is still producing cars at Ryton outside the city, the Hillman, Humber and Singer names have followed scores of other Coventry companies into oblivion.

gine, which was offered alongside the re-vamped V12. It was not to be until 1988 that the factory marketed its own covertible version of the XJ-S, thirteen years after the model first appeared.

Jaguar returned to the private sector in 1984 and, two years later, came the highly praised new XJ6 saloon. Then at the 1988 Birmingham Motor Show, the firm unveiled a superb mid-engined show stopper in the shape of the one-off V12-powered four-wheel-drive XJ220 supercar. Although there was talk of it entering production, by September of 1989 Sir John Egan confirmed that if it was to reach manufacturing status, it would have to be powered by the 3.5-litre twin turbo-charged V6 engine developed to replace the V12 in the firm's group C racers. This would involve redesigning the entire car and creating an altogether smaller one. By contrast, the Jaguar F-type sports car, the E's spiritual successor, is now said to be waiting in the wings. Intended to enter production in 1993, it is hoped that the new model will help to push Jaguar's output from approximately 50,000 cars per annum to around the 70,000 mark.

Work on the project began in the early 1980s though did not gain momentum until after the 1986 launch of the XJ6 saloon. Working under the direction of chief stylist Geoff Lawson, Keith Helfet, who has the lines of the XJ220 to his credit, is also responsible for those of the 2 + 2 F-type which, it is thought, will be available in coupe and detachable Targa top forms (XJ41) and as a convertible (XJ42). Unofficial photographs show strong visual associations to its distinguished predecessor, with a similarly shaped air intake and nose section to those of the E-type. With an apparent overall length of 15ft 1in (4.6m) and 6ft 1in (1.85m) wide, the F is slightly shorter but wider than the ultimate Series III E, the respective dimensions of which were 15ft 4in (4.86m) and 5ft 6in (1.68m).

At the heart of the new car is the 4-litre version of the AJ6 engine, introduced in 1989 for the XJ6 saloon. For this reason it was fitted with a forged, rather than the 3.6-litre's cast-iron crankshaft, for the top line 160mph (257kph) 350bhp twin turbo-charged F-type. This is used in conjunction with a four wheel drive system developed by Jaguar's close neighbour and FWD pioneer, FF Developments. The basic and more popular version of the F-type would be offered in unturbocharged rear wheel drive form.

By mid-1989 experimental cars were being evaluated in both Italy and Britain, with 'scoop' photographs being published in September by *Car* and *Autocar* magazines.

Jaguar's future was suddenly resolved on 31 October 1989, when Secretary of State for Trade and Industry, Nicholas Ridley, unexpectedly revealed that the government was waiving its Golden Share in the company – which limited any individual to a fifteen per cent holding – and this had been scheduled to expire at the end of 1990. This permitted Ford – which six weeks previously had announced its intention to build up its shareholding to the permitted level – to make an attractive all-out £1.6 billion bid for Jaguar, ahead of its General Motors rival. The latter had contemplated taking a minority holding in the company and was favoured by Sir John Egan but, on 2 November, the Jaguar board of directors recommended its acceptance of the Ford offer. This was subsequently approved by the firm's shareholders.

Jaguar today, after fifty-eight years as a British company (though a small one by international standards) is American-owned. But the reality may be that this will permit new models to be developed. The XJ200 project has been given the green light and the F-type cannot be far behind. After nearly arriving in 1970, this long-awaited sports car could take to the road nearly twenty years after its illustrious forebearer ceased production.

7 Buying the Right E-type

'Blessed is he that expects nothing, especially where second hand motors are concerned.'
Max Pemberton in *The Amateur Motorist*, 1907

It will be apparent that it was the twin appeals of performance and magnificent lines that sold the E-type when it was new. Although still a respectable performer, the E's looks can still turn heads but they can also be a trap for the unwary! The purpose of this chapter is to weigh up the pros and cons of the various models. Then when you have to decide which is the car for you, how you go about evaluating a good example, first by examining it and then, if it is drivable, taking it on the road.

But first it is probably appropriate to remind ourselves of the various models in the E-type range, all of which, apart from the 2 + 2 coupe, are available in roadster and fixed head coupe forms.

1961–1964	3.8-litre (Series I)
1964–1968	4.2-litre (Series I)
1966–1968	4.2-litre 2 + 2 coupe (Series I)
1968–1971	4.2-litre (Series II)
1968–1971	4.2-litre 2 + 2 coupe (Series II)
1971–1973	5.3-litre V12 2 + 2 coupe (Series III)
1971–1975	5.3-litre roadster V12 (Series III)

So of all these cars, which are the most sought after models? I will refrain from quoting prices because they will become outdated between my writing these words and the book appearing, such is the volatility of the classic car market. However, some trends for the E-type are already discernible. One is that, like most older cars, the convertible body tends to fetch rather more than the closed version. At the time of writing, summer 1989, the open 3.8-litre car is at about level pegging with its V12 equivalent though the latter looks all set to overtake it and will probably become *the* E-type to own in the next decade. Next come their respective closed versions. Then there is the Series I 4.2-litre roadsters of 1964–1968, followed by the V12 fixed-head coupe, and the Series II roadster, then the fixed-head coupes, starting with the 1961–1964 3.8-litre. Cinderella of the range is, ironically, the most practical and popular E-type of its day and that is the Series I and II 4.2-litre 2 + 2s which, of course, are only available in fixed-head forms.

So let's take a closer look at the respective advantages and disadvantages of the various models.

THE 3.8-LITRE (1961–1964)

There is little doubt, from a visual standpoint, that both this and its pre-1967 Series I successor, were visually the most impressive of the E-type model line-up. They are easily identifiable by their thin, tapering front and rear bumpers, modestly sized frontal air intake and headlamps contained behind perspex covers.

As far as the interior of the 3.8-litre cars is concerned, they have the handsome aluminium-finished central dashboard with black-faced instruments, which are particularly easy to read, while the centrally-positioned head and side light switch, a feature of all Jaguars of the day, has a distinctly pre-war feel to it if you like that sort of thing! Similarly there is a separate ignition key and starter button, a feature which harks back to the firm's pre-war days. An original Radiomobile radio, which was set in the central console, below the ashtray is an obviously desirable extra. The aluminium was perpetuated on the transmission tunnel though was subsequently changed to a black vinyl finish.

This brings us back to the seats. The leather-trimmed buckets came in for plenty of contemporary criticism as being uncomfortable though don't forget that the steering column is adjustable for reach by a knurled nut and rake is courtesy of a moveable slide and lock nut located alongside the column. There is also that identifiably 'Jaguar' wood-rimmed steering-wheel.

All these features relate to the roadster and fixed head coupe though each have their respective advantages and disadvantages. Probably none of us need converting to the joys of open air motoring – providing the weather is fine. The E-type's mohair hood, which was made by Jaguar in its trim shop, is reasonably easy to erect and keeps the weather out, to some extent! A popular fitment for the roadster was a glass fibre

The 2 + 2 tends to be the Cinderella of the E-type range, despite its practicality and popularity when new. This is probably because of some dilution of the coupe's lines and a modest falling-off in performance. One to watch perhaps?

Even the most ardent E-type enthusiast would concede that the roadster's hood may leave something to be desired. The glass fibre hard-top, shown on this 1964 car, is a desirable optional extra. But in colder weather, de-misting can become something of a problem.

hard-top, available from March 1962, which is secured to the top of the windscreen by three over centre catches and makes for a snug interior. The problem is that it immediately underlines the car's limited demisting arrangements, never a Jaguar strong point, a shortcoming which was not rectified, and then not truly satisfactorily, until the V12 acquired a rudimentary system in 1972. Don't expect to get too much luggage in the roadster's shallow boot. Beneath the floor is the spare wheel, and alongside it, the kidney-shaped petrol tank.

The fixed-head coupe, by contrast, is a far more practical car for round the year motoring and, I must confess, that I personally

find its lines superior to those of the open car. Luggage accomodation is obviously superior with a 4ft (1.22m) long and 3ft (0.91m) wide storage space, plus the convenience of a rear opening door.

So much for the 3.8's visual pros and cons but what about its mechanical peccadillos? As mentioned earlier in the book, its top speed is more likely to be approaching the 140mph (225kph) mark, with the aerodynamically superior coupe having the edge on the open car, rather than the 150mph (241kph) attained by the 1961 road test cars. The 3.8's 4.2-litre successor should record about the same top speed though with improved acceleration. The real limitation of the 3.8-litre cars is their Moss gearbox

As with most collectable cars, the E-type tends to be more sought-after in roadster than in coupe form. This is a 1962 car and therefore a 3.8-litre model.

which was also adversely commented upon when the E-type was new, so you can imagine what it's going to be like twenty or so years on! By this time synchromesh will probably be poor and the box does not lend itself to fast gear changes while first and reverse gears may be excessively noisy. So this is a drawback on the 3.8 – if you intend to do a lot of driving. Another shortcoming, which will only become apparent if the car is used a lot at night, is its relatively poor headlights with beams diluted by diffusion and scatter. The Series I 4.2s, which were fitted with

sealed beam units, are superior in this respect while the Series II cars, with their aesthetically instrusive lamps, are even better. Series I and II cars also benefited from the fitment of an alternator to replace the long suffering dynamo, which never really seemed to be up to the job. Early E-types also have a tendency to overheat in heavy traffic, which is particularly noticeable in the coupe. You have been warned!

Yet another shortcoming that will only become apparent on a test drive, is the relative inefficiency, certainly by present day standards, of the Dunlop bellows type servo and its attendant discs. The 4.2-litre cars were fitted with the greatly improved Lockheed in-line unit and thicker discs. Some 3.8s have been converted to the later servo in view of the fact that spares are extremely difficult to find for the Dunlop original.

The same also goes for the original Lucas immersed centrifugal impeller petrol pump, which has often been converted to the more conventional external unit, similar to that employed on the 4.2. This followed the factory issuing a conversion kit for the 3.8 in the early 1970s for the fitment of an SU type AUF 301 diaphragm pump. It was located on the right-hand side of the spare wheel well, alongside the wheelarch.

However, on the debit side, a neglected open example will probably require more radical restoration, because it is more vulnerable to the elements than a closed one.

*A 1967 'Series I½' perhaps offers the best of both worlds in that
it retains the attractive visual attributes of the Series I and the
exposed and improved headlamps of the Series II. This is an
America-sourced roadster pictured at the Montreal-based Expo 67.*

THE 4.2 LITRE (1964–1968)

This was externally very similar to the 3.8 so the same remarks therefore apply. The big changes were inside the car. There is no doubt that the new seats, which replaced the original bucket ones, were a great improvement on their predecessors. They are finished in pleated leather, are wider and more deeply upholstered, can be tilted forward, which allows easier access to the rear of the car, and are also adjustable for rake. Although the dashboard layout remained unchanged, the aluminium dash panel did produce some undesirable reflection and was replaced by a black finished panel though the instruments do not stand out quite so well. As already mentioned, acceleration is a noticeable improvement on that of the 3.8, and interestingly petrol consumption is slightly better. But the greatest improvement relates to the all-synchromesh gearbox, which was fitted right across the Jaguar range for the 1965 season. The advantages of the improved headlights have already been mentioned, so perhaps in many respects, the Series I 4.2 combines looks, performance *and* comfort, unless you happen to be the right shape for the 3.8!

THE 2 + 2 (1966–1968)

It is ironic that the family man's E-type fetches the least money of any car in the range though undoubtedly its rather high lines make it visually inferior to the equivalent fixed-head coupe. On the plus side, as it were, is obviously the rear seat though it is only really suitable for carrying children over long distances. Conversely there is increased weight, fuel consumption and a slightly clipped top speed. Also remember that automatic transmission, a Borg-Warner Model 8 three-speed gearbox, was introduced with this model, which flew in the face of the sports car concept, with once again a dilution of both performance and fuel consumption. We should not overlook the so-called Series I½ of 1968, which features the usual 4.2-litre exterior, with the exception of the improved, open, forward-mounted headlights.

THE SERIES II (1968–1971)

These are immediately identifiable by their enlarged air intake, with thickened-up bar containing the Jaguar badge, and exposed headlights. The small sidelight/flasher units were replaced by larger forward-mounted units located below the bumpers. At the rear, ugly rectangular casings located below the back bumper took the place of the earlier neat rear light/flashers. There were also new spoked wheels with a forged centre hub and straight spokes. Radial tyres were fitted as standard.

The interior benefited from the new safety conscious tumbler switches, and a combined steering-column lock and ignition key although, it has to be said, these combine to produce some dilution of personality.

Under the bonnet, you can easily identify these Series II cars by their matt black cam boxes, with aluminium fluting, while the twin electric fans are another recognition point. Incidentally, if you're faced with the prospect of an export left-hand drive version of the E-type, remember that it may be fitted with air conditioning, a facility that was not available on the right-hand drive cars because the unit was obstructed by the steering-column. So it cannot be converted back to right-hand drive, not a particularly difficult job but you've then got a non-original car, without sacrificing this facility. Performance of the Series II was slightly inferior to that of the I and this particularly applies to the American specification cars, the top speed of which was effectively strangled by its de-toxing equipment. You cannot expect much more than 120mph (193kph) from such a Series II.

THE SERIES III (1971–1975)

Compared with the pre-1971 E-type, the V12 Series III generation of 1971–1975 is visually different, particularly if an example is placed alongside a six. There are many who prefer the proportions of the pre-1971 E-type though no doubt there are plenty of V12 enthusiasts to challenge this viewpoint! Apart from having the wheelbase of the 2 + 2, it also has a wider track. The enlarged front air intake is a distinctive feature with, for the first time, a chromed grille and an additional air duct below. It was also good-bye to the handsome spoked centrelock wheels, mourned by many, and replaced by the chromed disc ones with fatter profiles and extended wheelarches. However, you should remember that wires were available at extra cost, so if you're contemplating a V12 with spoked wheels, this is perfectly in order.

Obviously under the bonnet, you won't be in any doubt that you're greeted by twelve cylinders. As far as top speed is concerned, this is about the same as the 4.2 at around

The 3.8-litre coupe is probably marginally faster than the open car in view of its better aerodynamics, not that you'd be able to prove it in Britain though!

The coupe has the advantage of extra carrying capacity over the roadster, plus impressive looks, as this 1964 car shows.

CPF 555B

A magnificent 1971 Series II coupe. This Series of the 1968–1971 era tends to be slightly cheaper than its Series I predecessors though the margin is a narrow one.

Once again the E-type coupe, of whatever year, scores as far as carrying capacity is concerned.

140mph (225kph). But you'll soon feel the benefit of the improved acceleration; that magnificent turbine-like performance which is unique to V12 power. On the debit side, they'll be high fuel consumption, about 14mpg or less, with the popular automatic version being even thirstier. The HE version of the V12 was still some years away. Also remember that ultimately you face a big engine repair bill if the car has done a high mileage. Fortunately the V12 is a strong, reliable unit and will cover at least 100,000 miles (160,000km) before it needs overhaul but when the time comes, be prepared for a big bill. This is not because the

power unit is excessively complicated. It isn't. It's just that there's about two of everything to replace or recondition!

You'll also have the benefit of power steering as a standard fitment on the Series III though some drivers complain that it is too light and lacks the assurance of road responses through the smaller leather, rather than big wood-rimmed wheel. The post-1972 cars have an additional appeal because of their improved fresh air facility and if you opt for a roadster with a hard-top, it is fitted with its own air outlet, which went some way to curing the model's ongoing demisting problems.

A 1968 left-hand drive Series II coupe. Note the repeater flashers on the sides of the front and rear wings, earless hubcaps and driver's wing mirror.

A fixed-head coupe Series III underlines the practicality of the V12-powered coupe in bad weather, as this example, pictured on a rainy day in the highlands of Scotland, demonstrates.

EVALUATION

So far so good but now we come to the potentially tricky business of evaluating the worth of a particular example. But before looking at the specific areas to check, I cannot overstate the point that the total restoration of an E-type is not a proposition for the amateur. This is mainly because of its sophisticated and unique body construction with its central tub and triangulated front section. One of the main difficulties is that, in the process of replacing the rusted parts, the originals have to be removed which will then weaken the monocoque and, more significantly, the hull may move slightly out of true. For a thorough structural re-build, the shell has to be mounted in a special jig to keep it in alignment. Also remember that some of the individual body panels were concealed by leading, so you'll see the importance of recognising your own limitations.

From the mechanical standpoint, although the overhaul of the six-cylinder XK engine is probably within the capabilities of the competent amateur, the same cannot be said for its independent rear-suspension. But on balance, you should be on the lookout for a car with a good body/frame and regard the mechanicals as secondary. Nowadays, it's almost impossible to find an E-type that hasn't rusted to some extent, so be on your guard! Yet another problem is that an E-type with a bad case of tin worm can be smartened up to look perfectly respectable. If you don't want to get caught, read on...

The Bodywork

As the condition of the E's bodywork is your prime consideration, make this your first port of call. Beginning at the front of the car, carefully examine that magnificent but vulnerable front bonnet and wing assembly. Start by gently tapping it around the front

Usually, cars that have been extensively modifed tend to be worth less than their perfectly standard contemporaries. Richard Essame's Chevrolet V8-powered E-type of 1971 shows a particularly high standard of conversion work, so this car would have some value in its own right.

The most collectable of E-types? A 1974 Series III roadster and one of the last fifty to be built.

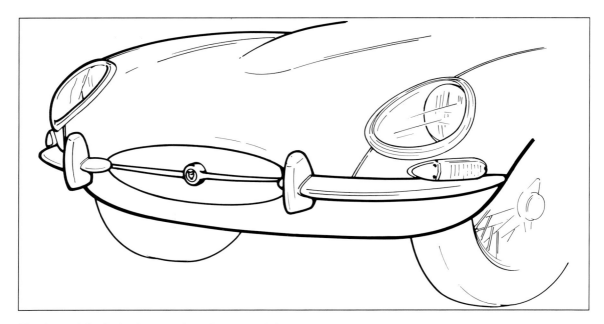

The front of the Series I 3.8- and 4.2-litre cars of the 1961–1967 era.

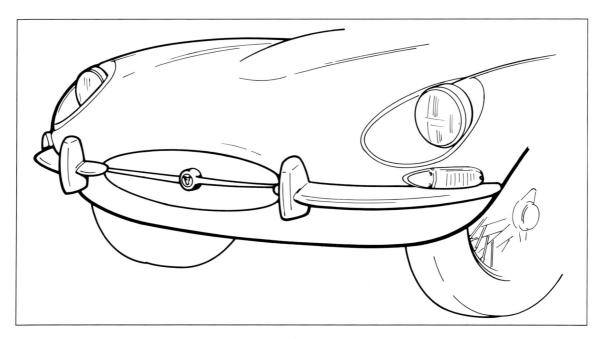

The 1967–1968 'Series I½' E-type, which retained the Series I bumpers, and air intake but featured the exposed headlamps of the Series II.

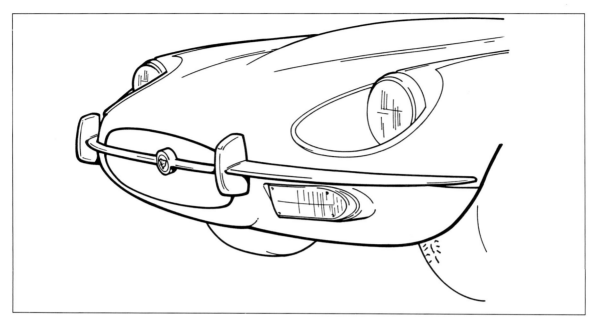

The Series II cars, made between 1968 and 1971, with full-width bumpers, enlarged air intake and bigger sidelight/flasher units relocated beneath the bumper.

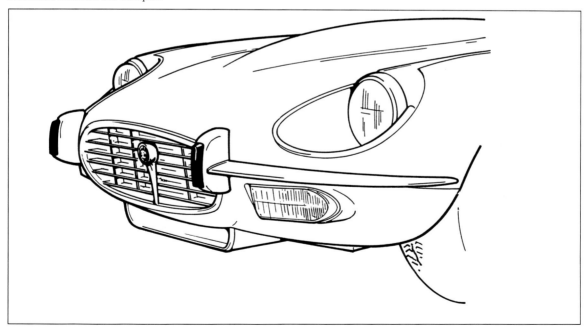

The Series III models of 1971–1975 are easily distinguished by their chromium-plated grille, with air intake below.

end. A deep resonance will indicate the presence of filler and you can confirm this by opening it and checking for dents. You may disturb some rust in the lower front nose section which may indicate the advanced decomposition of the panel underneath. Another vulnerable point is on the top of the wings, alongside the chrome strips which mask the joints between them and the centre section of the bonnet. Have a look at the underside of these joints while you've got the bonnet open. If there is rust topsides, the chances are that it will be even worse underneath with the flanges having rusted away. After you've taken a close look at the bonnet, stand back and see how well it appears to blend in with the rest of the car. If the alignment is poor, it might be an indicator of some long forgotten accident though it could have been badly refitted after its removal for

a more innocent reason. The bonnet is adjustable in practically every plane with the hinges shimmed to provide a precise join. Incidentally, replacing a bonnet after it has been removed is a job that could even take a professional restorer a couple of days to complete.

Moving back to the main central tub, you should carefully examine the sills. The originals were spot-welded in position but, if they have been replaced at some time in the car's life, they will be continuously welded or brazed. Their condition is a good indicator of the general condition of the car's hull. This particularly applies to the roadster, which hasn't the additional roof reinforcement provided by the coupe. The open car will flex badly if the sills are rusted or badly holed.

At the rear of the car, check the edges of

The hollow section sills lacked proper drainage or rust protection and quickly perforated at the bottom. Before buying, the area where the sill meets the floor under the car should be checked.

Almost invariably the sills will need replacing; here the outer ones on a 2 + 2 E-type have been removed and the rust damage to the floor/inner sill and the flitch plate adjacent to the rear wheel is very evident.

A similar area to that in the above picture is being restored on another car: note the new flitch plate and inner sill.

the rear wings and also underneath the car in the triangular area below the bumper and behind the wheel. The open car doesn't have an inner wing, so the apex of the wing proper is a favourite rust point. They do exist, however, on the coupe so closely examine the interior of the wings and around their edges for indications of corrosion.

At this point, have a look underneath the car and, with the aid of a powerful torch, examine the condition of the three strengthening ribs you'll see there. Check the nearby points where the rear-suspension radius arms are joined to the rear floor. This is a stress point and look out for rusting or for evidence of a botched repair. Either shortcoming is potentially dangerous. Also check the state of the hollow transverse beam you'll find beneath the seats.

Next open the boot, lift the Hardura matting if it is still present, and remove the spare wheel. Have a look at the well and also the point where the inner wing joins the floor. Another vulnerable area is around the rear number plate and the bodywork immediately above the twin exhaust pipes.

The doors too are not immune from corrosion. The danger area is where the outer skin joins its inner counterpart. In order to see whether rust has got a hold, grasp the lower edge of the door with your thumb on the outside of the door and try to flex the metal. If it produces a muted cracking noise, you'll know that all is far from well below the surface.

The Mechanicals

Now turn your attention to the car's mechanical aspects. Return to the front of the E-type, open the bonnet and carefully inspect the front framework for signs of rust or accident damage. Check for cracking in the vicinity of the joints. The frame itself isn't particularly prone to corrosion because of the presence of engine oil and vapour though it can suffer from spilled battery acid, par-

ticularly if its tray has disintegrated at some time. Therefore examine the frame in its immediate vicinity. Make a point of checking the bulkhead for evidence of denting, indicating signs of a bad crash, at the point where the frame is bolted to it. Also remember that you'll find the 3.8 and 4.2 cars' chassis plate on the front cross member above the damper mounting. If there isn't one, this might indicate that a new subframe has been fitted, perhaps the legacy of some long forgotten front end shunt. The Series III plate, by contrast, is to be found on the body of the car, under the bonnet, adjoining the bulkhead.

The first thing is to check that the E-type you are inspecting has its correct engine. It is not unknown for an earlier XK one, or a similar unit from the contemporary Mark X saloon, to have been fitted. Occasionally a 3.4-litre engine, with its less desirable pre-straightport head, might have been substituted and, the other day, I even heard of an XJ6-powered E-type! You'll find the engine number on the right-hand side of the block above the oil filter and also on the front of the cylinder head. They should correspond and, if they don't, it indicates that a replacement head has been fitted at some time. If the numbers do tally, they should also be the same as that shown on the data plate that you'll find on the sill on the off side of the engine compartment.

You'll only really be able to evaluate the condition of the car, and its engine, by driving it but don't be too alarmed if you're contemplating a 3.8 which looks as though it is suffering from an oil leak. Many do! The front-suspension is, by contrast, virtually trouble-free with wear often confined to the top and bottom ball joints. Alas, the same cannot be said for the rear-suspension, though this test is best reserved for when you drive the car, but some elements can be evaluated when the vehicle is stationary.

Worn splines are yet another potential hazard. If you are able to, loosen off the

Inner and outer wings meet at the rear to form a moisture trap,
and very often this much of the rear wing has to be replaced.

wheel nuts of both rear wheels. Then put the car in gear and apply the handbrake. Now jack the car up and place your hands at the nine and three o'clock positions. Move them within a limited arc. Any discernible movement will indicate that the splines are worn. You should also check the front wheels in a similar way though they don't normally suffer as much. You can also visually inspect the splines by removing the wheel in question completely. The splines should be flat on top, not pointed, which indicates undesirable wear.

But to revert to the rear end. A leaking differential is a fairly common E-type failing. This is usually caused by the inboard disc brakes overheating, which is conveyed to the differential, damaging the oil seals in the process. As the drive shafts do double duty as the top suspension link, this also puts additional stress on the long-suffering seals. As a result, lubricant gets on to the inside faces of the discs, to the ultimate detriment of the brakes. Yet another contributory factor is the pressure which can also build up in the differential assembly because of a blocked breather.

If the seals have failed, then you're faced with the problem of dismantling the entire-rear-suspension system which, although not particularly complicated, is not a job for the first-former. The diff unit itself is attached

An E-type's floor, and the bulkheads at either end, are all prone to rot. The bulkheads can usually be repaired but the floor is normally best replaced.

to the body by large Metalastik mountings. To check that these all-important components haven't separated, jack the car up and place it on axle stands positioned on the two longitudinal body members. Position the jack under the differential. Then lower the jack slightly. The differential should remain in position. if it moves appreciably, then you're in trouble. Don't worry, it can't fall out as it's held in place by the propellor shaft and anti-roll bar. Other wear points are the bottom pivot bearings on the rear stub axle carriers, the inner needle roller bearings on the inboard end of the wishbones and the anti-roll bar mountings and bushes.

It is also worth checking the steering,

evaluating it in a stationary position. The rack and pinion layout isn't particularly prone to wear and if there is some slack in the steering it might be the result of wear in the two universal joints in the steering-column. It could also be the result of worn rack mounting bushes.

While you're looking inside the car, check under the carpets to see whether some 'butcher' has carved the floor around the transmission tunnel to detach the gearbox from the engine. This is because an E-type clutch only has a life of about 30,000 miles (48,279km) and the engine/gearbox unit has to be removed to replace it. Such surgery means that the engine could remain in situ, so be on the lookout for it.

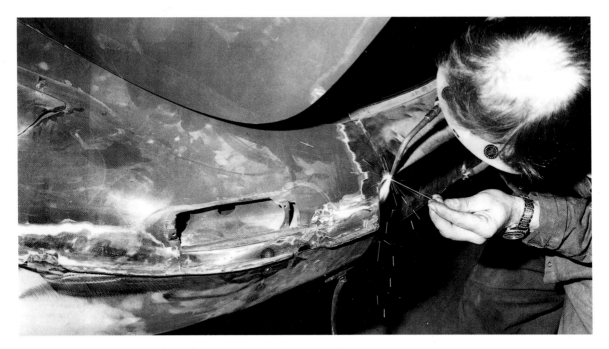

The area around the rear number-plate panel is another place subject to corrosion; here a new section is being let-in beneath a fixed-head's rear hatch opening.

After repairs have been completed, the seams need to be lead-filled and filed, just as they were at the factory.

Make a point of closely examining the condition of the car's interior. The leather seats, in particular, can be expensive to have renovated and repaired. Also if the car you are contemplating has been neglected, then the inside of a coupe will inevitably be in better condition than a roadster, which is more vulnerable to exposure to the elements.

Driving the E-Type

Now for the drive itself. The XK engine should start readily enough and quieten down within a minute or two. However, some tappet noise is not undesirable. Once the engine has reached its operating temperature, check the oil pressure gauge. 40psi at 3,000rpm is an acceptable figure and be particularly suspicious of any reading below 30. The clutch has a fairly long travel and will only begin to take up rather late in the day. Don't get caught unawares by the high first gear, so you might experience some difficulty in getting a smooth take-off. You'll also find that first is noisy on the 3.8-litre. This is quite normal but be more suspicious of grating or grinding. Gearbox repairs can be expensive and replacement parts aren't cheap.

Be prepared for the poor brakes on the 3.8, which weren't really up to the job when the car was new, so twenty or so years on they're not likely to be very impressive and will very much depend on the condition of the servo. You'll need a strong right foot! The rack and pinion steering is a delight and you'll certainly be impressed by its precision and, above all, its lightness.

The six is a strong, reliable unit and quite capable of exceeding 100,000 miles (160,930km) between overhauls. The best way of evaluating its condition is to drive around in top gear at about 40 to 50mph (64 to 80kph) for a time and then sharply depress the accelerator. If the engine is in a good state, you should only be able to see a light exhaust haze in the rear view mirror. If, on the other hand, there are clouds of blue smoke, the car is suffering from excessive bore wear.

Now come the all-important checks on that potentially troublesome independent rear-suspension. Make a point of listening out for clunks or clicks, as a result of backing the accelerator pedal on and off. This could indicate a variety of maladies, including worn universal half-shaft joints, slack in the rear splines or wear in the bottom pivots of the stub axles. Be aware of a tendency for the car to steer from the rear. If this shortcoming is apparent, it is probably caused by the worn differential mountings mentioned earlier.

But finally a word of warning. Don't be tempted to put your foot down hard on the accelerator as the E-type's legendary performance can catch you unawares, particularly because the car's speed can be deceptive. So don't overdo it.

Much the same remarks apply to the Series III V12-powered cars, with the exception of the engine. Like the six, it is a robust and untemperamental unit. Before starting the engine, grasp the water pump pulley and see if there is any undesirable slack present. Once you've started it, listen out for a rattle from the front of the engine, which may indicate a worn timing chain. This is a particular problem associated with the V12 and some engines have been known to display this malady after only covering 35,000 miles (56,325km). You're listening for the chain rubbing on the timing chest, particularly while revving up and on the over-run. In addition, keep your ears open for any bearing rattles as worn shells may not show up by a low reading on the oil pressure gauge. This should, incidentally, be not less than 60psi at 3,500rpm.

Be suspicious of an engine that has suffered recent water loss. The V12 is a little prone to overheating, a shortcoming that was often caused by a failure of the thermostatically-controlled fan to operate. This could result in a blown cylinder head gasket, or gaskets, and if this was not attended to, the heads could weld themselves to the block. Not a pleasant thought! A misfire usually relates to problems with the OPUS electronic ignition system.

After you've driven the car, park it and subsequently move it and check for oil leaks. The V12 is a little prone to wear in the crankshaft oil seal, which can deposit lubricant at around the point where the engine joins the gearbox bellhousing. Although the new seal itself is not expensive, the engine has to be removed to fit it, which is.

Buying an E-Type

If you've set your heart on an E-type, there doesn't seem to be any shortage of examples, so it is well worth shopping around. A perusal of the classified advertising columns of the specialist motoring press in such magazines as *Classic Cars, Classic and Sportscar, Practical Classics, Motor Sport* and *Jaguar Quarterly* is well worthwhile, don't overlook the weekly *Exchange and Mart* and even your local newspaper.

It is also well worth going along to a meeting organised by one of the Jaguar clubs. There you'll be able to talk to enthusiasts about their cars and the snags involved in running and restoring them. This brings us to parts availability, which is also considered in the next chapter.

JAGUAR E-TYPE
3.8-LITRE 1961–1964
PRINCIPAL MODIFICATIONS

Chassis nos. begin Open Two-Seater (OTS), RHD from 850001/LHD 875001
Chassis nos. begin Fixed-Head Coupe (FHC), RHD from 860001/LHD 885001

August 1961
LHD/RHD
(OTS 850048/875133) Front wheel hubs, introduction of water shields

October
(OTS 850092/875386, FHC 86005/885021) Higher output dynamo. New bonnet catches located inside car

January 1962
(OTS 850291/876130, FHC 860033/885210) Mintex brake pads adopted in place of M 40 linings

May
(FHC) Electrically heated rear window option available
(OTS) Hard-top available

June
(OTS 850358/876582, FHC 860176/885504) Heel wells introduced in front floor
(FHC 860479/886014) Modified tail lamps

October
Rear axle ratio changed to 3.31:1 on US and Canadian cars and to 3.07:1 on UK and other markets

June 1963
(OTS 850722/879494, FHC 861185/888706-UK) Mintex M59 brake pads adopted. Thickness of rear disc increased. Modified differential unit

September
(OTS 850737/879821, FHC 861226/889003) 3.31:1 rear axle ratio introduced for UK market

November
(OTS 850768/880291) Boot lock modified, following breakage of interior cable. New lock operated through hole in number plate panel

March 1964
(OTS 850809/880840, FHC 861446/889787) Interior door trim modified to improve appearance and ease of fitting

March
(Engine no. RA–4975) Full flow oil-filter introduced

April
(Engine no. RA 5735) E-type and Mark II cylinder heads commonised

May
(Engine no. RA 5801) Diaphragm clutch introduced

*The V12-engined roadster, without its hard-top, and
appreciating.*

JAGUAR E-TYPE
4.2-LITRE (Series I) 1964–1968
PRINCIPAL MODIFICATIONS

Chassis nos. begin Open Two-Seater (OTS),
RHD 1E.1001/LHD 1E.10001
Chassis nos. begin Fixed-Head Coupe (FHC),
RHD 1E.2001/LHD 1E.30001
Chassis nos. begin Fixed-head Coupe (2 + 2)
RHD 1E.50001/LHD 1E.75001

June 1965
LHD/RHD
(OTS 1E.1152/1E.10703, FHC 1E.20329/
1E.30772) 3.07:1 final drive ratio on cars
adopted for all countries, except North
America which are fitted with 3.54:1 ratio
(OTS 1E.1226/1E.10958, FHC 1E.20612/
1E.30912) Aperture on right-hand side of
gearbox side panel to give access to
speedometer drive

September
(OTS 1E.1253/1E.11049, FHC 1E.20692/
1E.31078) Revised oil breather fitted

November
(FHC 1E.20852/1E.31413) Self locking rear
door prop introduced
(Engine No. 7E.5170) Felt oil-filter replaced
by paper element

March 1966
(OTS 1E.1413/1E.11535, FHC 1E.20993/
1E.31765) Seven tooth pinion fitted to
steering gear in place of eight tooth one
previously employed
(OTS 1E.1409/1E.11715, FHC 1E.20978/
1E.32009) Dunlop SP.41 HR tyres fitted
(OTS 1E.1413/1E.11741, FHC 1E.21000/
1E.32010) Rear bumper fixing accessible
from exterior of car. Hitherto only accessible
from petrol tank and spare wheel area

September
(OTS 1E.1479/1E.12580, FHC 1E.21228/
1E.32632) Bonnet and front wings, bumpers
and heater intake commonised with 2 + 2
models

December
(OTS 1E.1545/1E.12965, FHC 1E.21335/
1E.32888) Exhaust down pipes fitted with
heat shield

July 1968
(Engine nos. 7E.13501 and 2 + 2, 7E.53582)
Laycock clutch replaced by Borg and Beck
diaphragm spring clutch 2 + 2 1E.50875/
1E.77407 Larger diameter torsion bars
(OTS 1E.1814/1E.15487, FHC 1E.21518/
1E.34339, 2 + 2 1E.50912/1E.77475)
Chrome wire wheels fitted with forged hub
(OTS 1E.1853/1E.15753, FHC 1E.21579/
1E.34458, 2 + 2 1E.50972/1E.77602) Silver
painted wire wheels fitted with forged hub

JAGUAR E-TYPE 4.2-LITRE (Series II)
1968–1971
PRINCIPAL MODIFICATIONS

Chassis nos. begin Open Two-Seater (OTS),
RHD 1R.1001/LHD 1R.7001
Chassis nos. begin Fixed-Head Coupe (FHC),
RHD 1R.20001/LHD 1R.25001
Chassis nos. begin Fixed-Head Coupe (2 + 2),
RHD 1R.35001/LHD 1R.40001

December 1968
(OTS 1R.1085, FHC 1R.20095, 2 + 2
1R.35099) Steering lock on RHD cars

January 1969
LHD/RHD
(OTS 1R.1013/1R.7443, FHC 1R.20007/
1R.25284, 2 + 2 1R.35011/1R.40208) Lucas
11AC alternator introduced with side entry
cables

March
(OTS 1R.1054, FHC 1R.20073, 2 + 2,
1R.35099) Non-eared hub caps fitted to RHD
cars, bring them into line with LHD cars
(OTS 1R.1068/1R.7993, FHC 1R.20119/
1R.25524, 2 + 2 1R.35798/1R.40668)
Modifications to upper panel of petrol tank

April
(OTS 1R.9860, FHC 1R.26533, 2 + 2
1R.42382) Ignition/starter switch with load
shedding facility introduced on LHD cars

May
(OTS 1R.1138/1R.8869, FHC 1R.20212/
1R.26005) Perforated leather trim and
improved head rests introduced

June
(OTS 1R.118/1R.9570, FHC 1R.20270/
1R.26387, 2 + 2 1R.35353/1R.42118) Gas
filled bonnet stay, replacing spring

August
(Engines nos. 7R.6306 and 7R.38106) New
position for engine number, being stamped
on crankcase bell housing flange adjacent to
dip stick on left-hand side of engine

October
(OTS 1R.1351/1R.10537, FHC 1R.24425/
1R.26835, 2 + 2, 1R.35564/1R.42677)
Battery operated clock introduced to replace
mercury cell unit

November
(Engines nos. 7R.8688, 7R.8855) New
camshafts with redesigned profiles

May 1970
(2 + 2 1R.35816/1R.43924) Handbrake revised
with longer lever and angled end

August
(OTS 1R.1776, FHC 1R.20955) Larger
diameter torsion bars on RHD cars

December
(Engine no. 14269) Suffix letters introduced
following engine number to denote
compression ratio: H – High Compression, S
– Standard Compression, L – Low
Compression

JAGUAR E-TYPE 5.3-LITRE
(Series III) 1971–1975
PRINCIPAL MODIFICATIONS

Chassis nos. begin Open Two-Seater (OTS),
RHD 1S1001/LHD 1S2001
Chassis nos. begin 2 + 2 RHD 1S50001/LHD
1S70001

November 1971
(OTS 1S.1093/1S.20099, 2 + 2 1S.50592/
1S.72332) 3.31:1 crown wheel and pinion
modified

December
(Engine no. 7S.4510) Crankshaft thrust
washer revised

(OTS 1S.1152/1S.20122, FHC 1S.50872/
1S.72357) Handbrake now common to LHD
and RHD cars

March
(OTS 1S.1163/1S.20135, 2 + 2 1S.50875/
1S.72450) Demister flap operated by cable
and connecting rods, instead of cable and
pinion previously employed

April 1972
3.07:1 axle ratio available as option on cars
with manual gearbox

May
(Engine no. 7S.6310) Lighter pistons
introduced

June
(OTS 1S.1348/1S.20569, 2 + 2 IS.51263/
1S.73372) Larger cam profile on torsion bar

(Engine no. 7S.7155) Shell bearings on big end
bearings modified to delete oil feed holes

October
(Engine no. 7S.7856) Oil feed in connecting
rod small end deleted

December
(OTS 1S.1443/1S.20921, 2 + 2 1S.51318/
1S.73372) Revised pinion valve on steering
gear.

February 1973
(Engine no. 7S.9715) Modified Borg-Warner
Model 12 gearbox, as available on XJ12
saloon, introduced

April
(OTS 1S.1663/1S.212606, 2 + 2 1S.51610/
1S.74266) Air ducts to rear brakes modified
to improve ground clearance and now fitted
at factory rather than by dealer

May
(Engine no. 7S.10799) Crankshaft, as fitted to
engine in V12 saloon, introduced

1974
(OTS 1S.23240, 2 + 2 1S.74586) Rubber
overriders introduced on cars destined for
American market

8 Spare Parts, Clubs and Specialists

'To say that the history of automobilism is that of its clubs is nearer the literal truth than a lapse into exaggeration.'

Charles L. Freeston in *Motors and Motor-Driving*, 1902

The enjoyment of restoring and maintaining any old car is, to a great extent, conditioned by the availability of spare parts. As far as the E-type is concerned, the earliest example was built back in 1961, so can you expect to obtain parts for what is now a relatively old car? The answer is an unequivocal 'yes'. One of the beneficial side effects of the recent escalation in E-type prices is that, in the main, the supply of spare parts is no longer a problem with the model. Having said that, there are some items that may prove to be a little tricky to obtain and may require some diligence to track down.

MECHANICAL COMPONENTS

Let's start with mechanical components, which have always tended to be in the best supply. These should be readily obtainable from specialist suppliers and it is even worth trying well established Jaguar dealers for such items as decoke sets, valves and hard-working parts like brake pads and discs, steering joints and clutch plates. This applies particularly to the V12-powered Series III cars, which were only discontinued in 1975.

The only item on the earlier cars that might prove to be tricky to obtain is an overhaul kit for the Dunlop bellows type brake servo on the 3.8-litre models though some detective work on your part will probably be able to locate one. The difficulty is that the Lockheed servo fitted to the subsequent 4.2-litre cars was much more efficient than the Dunlop unit, which required considerably more pedal pressure to bring the car to a halt. Here is an instance when you will have to decide whether you essentially want your E-type to drive, or have your eyes on concours competitions. In the latter instance, the accent is very much on originality, so if that is your preference, you'll have to opt for the Dunlop servo, despite its shortcomings.

You'll be faced with a similar predicament with the submersible petrol pump of the 3.8. This wasn't a particularly successful unit and was replaced by the externally-mounted pump of the 4.2. Many 3.8-litre owners have converted their cars to the latter pump and as it is usually positioned out of sight, you might get away with this modification, unless the concours judge happens to be particularly eagle-eyed!

The E-type hard-tops were produced at Jaguar's Radford works in the plant which, for a time, also made glassfibre bodies for the Daimler SP250 sports car.

A large rear window has always been an attribute of the hard-top E-type. This one is for a Series III car. They are, alas, only available second-hand and command high prices.

Similarly, a complete tool-kit is a sought-after objective. This one comes from a 1964 Series I E-type, though the material used on the Series II cars was of poorer quality.

BODY PARTS

From mechanical components, we come to body parts. These were the sort of items that used to hang around in Jaguar agents' spares stores for a time after a particular model went out of production, but then suddenly disappeared. Today, with very few exceptions, you can obtain practically every panel for the roadster and most for the fixed-head coupe. The exceptions are the roof and rear door for the latter and the absence of these important parts have resulted in some derelict coupes being rebuilt as roadsters. You have been warned! A word of caution about replacement body panels. Don't imagine that you can buy the part, and then immediately fit it to the car. However good, it will probably require some hand fitting and some careful welding which, in truth, is really a job for the professional.

A perfect illustration of this state of affairs is that replacement bonnets available for all E-types, apart from the Series I½, can even take a professional a good week to fit to the car. The reason is that the bonnet/wing assembly is not a single pressing but is made up of a number of them, so the alignment of the individual part in relation to that of its neighbour has to be resolved before the unit as a whole can be offered up to the car. But in general terms, the availability of such items does mean that the days of the badly rusted E-type having to be scrapped – because of the absence of body parts – is now over.

TRIM PARTS

This bringing us to what used to be the trickiest of replacement items: those of trim parts. That means interior items like seats and door coverings and body trim parts such as radiator grilles, badges and headlamp surrounds. Once again the specialist manufacturers have done E-type owners proud

and most items are available. Such is the ever changing state of spares availability that a long unobtainable item, the moulding on the surround of the fixed head coupe's rear door, which is a plastic rather than rubber material, is now available. It is details like this one that puts the right finishing touch to any good restoration.

As far as obtaining these parts is concerned, you'll find no shortage of firms advertising in the specialist press but your best guide is to talk to other enthusiasts to discover which are the most satisfactory companies, and the ones which offer the most competitively priced spares.

Just three established specialist suppliers which have a good selection of E-type parts are:

F B Components,
35–41 Edgeware Road, Marston,
Oxford OX3 OUA.

Norman Motors,
100 Mill Hill,
London NW6.

Martin Robey Sales,
Camp Hill Industrial Estate,
Pool Road,
Nuneaton CV10 9AE.

Robey also restore E-types, as do:

XK Engineering of Unit,
Netherwood Industrial Estate,
Radcliffe Road,
Atherstone CV9 3NX.

Colin Ford's C.F. Autos,
5 South Road, Erith,
Kent.

C.F. Autos have just completed the renovation of *Practical Classics'* fixed-head E-type.

There is no better way of getting to know the E-type than to attend a Jaguar rally and concours, such as this one.

BRITISH CLUBS

Yet another, and extremely important source and repository of information on spare parts, is the Jaguar car clubs. This is where joining a club is so important because you will not only be able to talk to fellow members about the best parts' sources but some clubs also have an active spares department which can also initiate the remanufacture of parts. So if you do decide to join the ranks of E-type owners, I would consider it absolutely essential to join one of the many Jaguar clubs.

Britain has three Jaguar clubs at present, the largest of which is the Jaguar Drivers' Club (JDC), which has about 12,500 members. The JDC is the spiritual successor of the pre-war SS Car Club which began life back in 1934. A national event was instigated in the following year, appropriately, at SS's Blackpool birth place though the day was clouded by the disappearance of the club's founder, C Moxon Cook, who departed with the members' money – William Lyons being left to pick up the bill at the Imperial Hotel. Not surprisingly at this time Lyons was all for scrapping the club, and publicity chief Bill Rankin was given the choice of forgetting about it, or running it himself! Manfully he decided to carry on and the SS club continued with, albeit unofficial

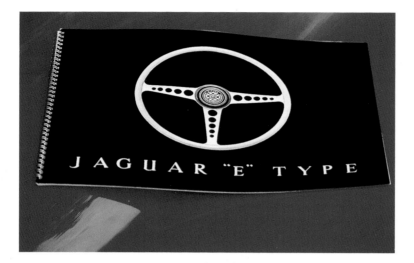

Original E-type sales brochures can be obtained from specialist dealers, at a price, while modern reprints are also available.

The precise alignment of the body panels on an E-type, as in this case, is both cosmetically and structurally important.

Obtaining the correct spare parts – in this instance a brake bleed pipe in its original tin – is a very real asset.

Rear tail-light clusters of the Jaguar E-type.

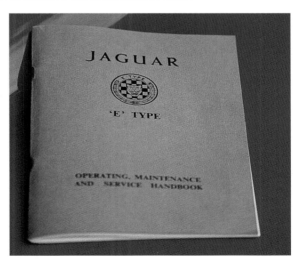

You may be lucky and obtain an original E-type handbook but, like the brochure, modern reproductions are available.

*The E-type is a pleasure to drive, whether in the
city ...*

factory involvement, until the outbreak of
the Second World War.

After the war came the change of the
company's name from SS to Jaguar and
Rankin became fully occupied with corporate affairs, so the club lapsed. It was not
until 1955 that it was reactivated, due to the
persistence of XK120 owner Raymond Play-
ford, who wrote to the motoring press, sug-
gesting a club for Jaguar owners. The in-
augural meeting of the Jaguar Drivers' Club
was held in May 1956 but the fur really
began to fly when the presidency was offered
to the recently knighted Sir William Lyons

and the factory responded by forbidding the
use of the Jaguar name in the club's title.
The SS Car Club debacle obviously still
rankled! But after lengthy negotiations, the
JDC agreed to the presence of two factory
representatives on its board of manage-
ment, an allocation that still continues to
this day.

Sir William Lyons subsequently accepted
the club's presidency and became a frequent
attender at many of its events, much to the
delight of the membership. Although initially
XK owners predominated, as the club has
grown it has opened to owners of *any* SS or

Jaguar car of any age. The individual models have their own registers (there are seven in all within the club) and the E-type one, which caters both for the six-cylinder and V12-engined cars, is the largest within the club.

Other advantages of membership include *Jaguar Driver*, a high quality monthly magazine containing technical information and a vast range of spares and services. There is advice from a technical expert, as well as a 'find-a-parts' scheme for particularly elusive spares. Monthly pub meetings are held. Forty-three of these meetings are spread throughout the country so there is

bound to be one near you. The big event of the year is National Day, usually held at a stately home, with SSs, Jaguars and, in particular E-types, as far as the eye can see! If you're interested in joining the JDC, then write to:

The General Secretary,
Jaguar Drivers' Club,
18 Stuart Street,
Luton LU1 2SL.

Up until 1985 the Jaguar Drivers' Club was the country's only national Jaguar club but, that year, there was a schism within the

... or in the country.

Such all-important items as this badge on the rear of a 3.8 are available in replica form.

organisation and the outcome was the Jaguar Enthusiasts' Club (JEC) which today has about 6,000 members. Like the JDC, the Jaguar Enthusiasts' Club caters for all SS and Jaguar models. The club offers a similar range of services, including a club insurance scheme, free technical advice, *Jaguar Enthusiast*, a monthly club magazine, along with a booklet of Specialist Services available to Jaguar owners. In addition, most of the Jaguar book titles are available and, as far as E-type owners are concerned, this includes 3.8, 4.2 and V12 workshop manuals, along with the respective parts catalogues.

There are no registers for individual models within the JEC but one of its most popular services is a Special Tool Department, aimed at those enthusiasts maintaining or restoring their own cars. E-type

owners will be interested to know that they can buy such useful aids to XK engine renovation as a crankshaft rear main bearing sizing tool, which also applies to the V12 unit. Then there is a timing chain adjuster, the camshaft setting plate, valve spring compressor and a valve gear storage board, particularly helpful if you're undertaking a decoke. A useful engine-lifting bracket is aimed for use on XK engines not fitted with lifting brackets. Specially manufactured spare parts are also available and although these mostly relate to the Mark II saloons which are so popular in the club, there is an E-type strapping kit used for securing the wiring loom to the front frame work or for containing the wires to the element of the heated rear window, if one is fitted, on the fixed-head coupe.

If you want to join the Jaguar Enthusiasts Club, write to:

> Lynn and Graham Searle,
> Sherborne,
> Mead Road,
> Stoke Gifford,
> Bristol BS12 6TS

In 1988 came yet another organisation, the Jaguar Car Club (JCC), and I can do no better than to quote from the club's application form, as it clearly sets down its services and objectives:

> 'Our club was founded at the beginning of 1988 with 100 Founder Members, at the initiative of a number of senior Jaguar owners. The need was felt for a "motoring" Jaguar car club, which would be strongly orientated towards using Jaguar models of all types and would be particularly active in racing, sprint and rally competition events. Above all, it would be a friendly organisation, where size would be of secondary consideration.'

The JCC publishes a quarterly magazine, *Jaguar World*, along with a monthly newsletter. It organises a full competition programme of race meetings, hill climbs, sprints and rallies as well as social events. The club does not stock spare parts but can invariably give helpful advice on where to get them.

The membership secretary of the Jaguar Car Club is:

> Richard Pugh,
> 19, Eldorado Crescent,
> Cheltenham GL50 2PY.

NORTH-AMERICAN CLUBS

Of course, the vast majority of E-types were exported to America and this is reflected by the forty or so Jaguar clubs there. These belong to the works supported Jaguar Clubs of North America which can be contacted at:

> 600 Willow Tree Road,
> Leonia,
> New Jersey 07605,
> USA.

OTHER CLUBS

There are also clubs, the world over, which cater for Jaguars of all ages, which naturally include the E-type. There are five or so Down Under in Australia and Switzerland boasts no less than four! European countries, such as France, Germany, Italy, Belgium and Holland all possess Jaguar clubs.

Finally, a word about what is essentially a club activity that has latterly cropped up in this book: the *concours*, or to give it its full name, the *concours d'élégance*. This is essentially a gathering of cars, which are then judged by a team of experts, who will probably have broken the car down into four principal divisions: bodywork including boot, engine, interior and underside. They will be evaluating the car from a standpoint of its condition and originality on the day. This means that the judging team will not be over-impressed by a car, the engine of which has been burnished with a frenzy usually associated with an army kit inspection! Similarly the car which has parts unnecessarily plated will be penalised. The criteria is that it should most closely resemble the state in which it left the factory and, as I mentioned earlier, if you are a 3.8-litre owner, this means having the original Dunlop servo, rather than the improved Lockheed one which was introduced on the 4.2.

But whatever your competitive preferences, the important thing is to enjoy driving your E-type. That is, after all what all cars, and Jaguars in particular, were designed for in the first place.

Bibliography

BOOKS

Berry, R. 1978. *Motor Racing and the Manufacturer*. Aztex.

Hassan, W. with Robson, G. 1975. *Climax in Coventry*. Motor Racing Publications.

King, P. 1989. *The Motor Men*. Quiller Press.

Porter, P. 1989. *Jaguar E-type: The Definitive History*. Haynes.

Robson, G. 1983. *Jaguar D-type and XKSS*. Osprey.

Skilleter, P. 1979. *The Jaguar E-type: A Collector's Guide*. Motor Racing Publications.

Skilleter, P. 1975. *Jaguar Sports Cars*. Haynes.

Whyte, A. 1987. *Jaguar Sports Racing and Works Competition Cars from 1954*. Haynes.

Whyte, A. 1980. *Jaguar: The History of a Great British Car*. Patrick Stephens.

Wood, J. 1988. *Wheels of Misfortune The Rise and Fall of the British Motor Industry*. Sidgwick and Jackson.

MAGAZINES AND PERIODICALS

(The) Autocar
Car and Driver
(The) Motor
Proceedings of the Institution of Automobile Engineers
Road and Track
World Car Catalogues, 1962–1974.

ARTICLES

Hassan, W. T. F. 1978. Jaguar V12 Engine – its Design and Background. *Technical, Administrative and Supervisory Section of the AUEW*.

Lyons, Sir William. 1969. The History of Jaguar and the Future of the Specialist Car in the British Motor Industry. *Lord Wakefield Gold Medal Paper*.

Index

(Italic numbers refer to illustrations)